Mini-Books are designed to
inform and entertain you.

They cover a wide range of
subjects — from Yoga to Cat-Care:
from Dieting to Dressmaking:
from Spelling to Antiques.

Mini-Books are neat
Mini-Books are cheap
Mini-Books are exciting

COLLECTING ENGLISH COINS
1837–1971

is just one Mini-Book
from a choice of many

Recently published in Corgi Mini-Books

DAVID NASH of Temple Coins Ltd.

COLLECTING ENGLISH COINS
1837–1971

A MINI-BOOK BY CORGI

COLLECTING ENGLISH COINS
1837–1971

A MINI-BOOK   552 76346 2

PRINTING HISTORY
Mini-Book Edition published 1970
Copyright © 1970 by
Temple Numismatic Publications Ltd.

Mini-Books are published by Transworld Publishers Ltd.,
Bashley Road, London, N.W.10
Filmset in Photon Times 10 on 10½ pt. by
Richard Clay (The Chaucer Press), Ltd., Bungay, Suffolk
Printed in Great Britain by
Fletcher & Son Ltd., Norwich, Norfolk

CONTENTS

ACKNOWLEDGEMENTS

Illustrations supplied by Temple Numismatic Publications Ltd.

Illustrations on pages 11 and 21 are reproduced from *London Pictures* by the Reverend Richard Lovett, M.A., published by Lutterworth Press.

The Great Seal

CHAPTER I

VICTORIA 1837–1901

Victoria was born on 24th May 1819 at Kensington Palace, London. She was the only child of Edward, Duke of Kent, fourth son of George III and of Princess Victoria Mary Louisa of Saxe-Coburg-Gotha (widow of Prince Emich Karl of Leiningen, by whom she had two children). George III's children survived to number thirteen; his grandchildren were not so fortunate, all but two of them died in infancy. Of these two, Victoria was the elder and therefore nearer to the throne. The younger one was the Duke of Cambridge, Commander in Chief of the British Army for nearly forty years. By modern standards Victoria's upbringing would be considered a harsh one; but it prepared her well for her task to come.

On the death of William IV she became Queen on 20th

June 1837 and was crowned at Westminster on 28th June 1838. The Kingdom of Hanover passed then to her uncle, the disreputable and unpopular Duke of Cumberland, fifth son of George III, as, under Salic Law, a woman could not mount the throne of Hanover.

The familiar Wyon portrait used after 1860—this gave the coins the 'bun' nickname.

Victoria met Prince Albert four years before their marriage, which took place at St. James's Palace on 10th February 1840, an event which was to have a great influence on the Court, Parliament, and country, by its example of domestic virtue and devotion to duty. During her long reign, 1837–1901, she saw the appointment of twenty Prime Ministers, among them Gladstone, whom she disliked intensely, Disraeli, and Lord Salisbury, the longest in office. In the early part of her reign she undoubtedly leaned towards the Whigs, but in her later life she was happier with the Conservative ministries of Lord Salisbury. It may be said that her reverence for home and country, well displayed during the South African War, long out-lasted her notable reign and was an example passed on to all her subjects, regardless of class.

During those sixty-four years, 1837–1900, as the young girl-Queen matured into an European leader, so the British Empire expanded and flourished.

Victorian Coins

It is not commonly known, but there were more coins issued bearing Victoria's portrait than of any other ruler. There are three distinct divisions in the type of coinage issued during her reign, 'the Young-head', 'the Jubilee-head', and 'the Old-head'. Strictly speaking, there is a fourth type, the Gothic-bust, which for our purposes will be considered as part of 'the Young-head' group.

When the young Queen came on to the throne she was only eighteen years of age. William Wyon, the famous engraver, prepared the first 'Young-head' portrait, which was only to survive on a few of the English denominations until her golden jubilee in 1887.

William Wyon (1795–1851) was Chief Engraver at the Royal Mint from 1828 until 1851 and designed the famous City of London Medal, commemorating the young Queen's

One Penny Model. These unusual little pattern coins were produced by Joseph Moore of Birmingham in an effort to persuade the authorities to change from the heavy copper coins in current use. It is reported that they were made around 1848.

One Decimal Penny—the reverse of an extensive series of official patterns produced in or around 1859.

accession in 1837. It is interesting to note that this medal was adopted by Henry Corbould for the first postage stamps of 1840, among which featured the famous 1*d.* Black.

During the long reign several major coin changes were effected, the most notable being that bronze was substituted for copper metal, resulting in a completely redesigned

The elegant old-head obverse, used on all our coinage from 1895 to 1901, designed by Thomas Brock.

bronze coinage. At the same time the weights of the denominations were reduced. In 1887 gold and silver coinage was made to bear a new effigy of the Queen, known as the Jubilee Head; the bronze coins retained the Young Head design. Further, in 1893 the Old Head replaced the Jubilee Head, and all the coins changed their obverses.

The first coin issue circulated in 1838 included the sovereign, half-sovereign, crown, half-crown, shilling, sixpence, and fourpence. The first four denominations all displayed the new coat of arms on the reverses. Now that Britain had

15

severed its connection with Hanover, this shield was simplified by the omission of the central 'escutcheon of pretence'. On the half-sovereign the arms are shown in a more ornamental shield than on the other coins, and the surrounding wreath is omitted. The shilling, sixpence, fourpence, and Maundy coins all follow the reverses of William IV's reign; the first two having the amount in words surrounded by a wreath with the crown above and the date

The reverse of a brass political token known as a 'Cumberland Jack'. The specimen shown here has an 1830 date—completely erroneous, because it refers to the sending of the Duke of Cumberland to Hanover, after Victoria came to the throne in 1837. These tokens are of many types and dates and are very common.

below. The fourpenny piece, or groat, shows Britannia on the reverse. The crown piece did not appear until 1844, although a proof coin was struck in 1839, and is included in the proof set of that year. This proof specimen set is both very rare and, for the would-be-purchaser, very costly. It is particularly interesting, as it contains the classical five-pound piece by William Wyon, depicting the Queen as Una in the foreground, with a lion behind. All the remaining

An 1849 Groat—a rare instance of the Britannia design on a silver coin.

Una and the Lion pattern £5. One of the first series of official pattern-cum-proof coins issued in 1839 in limited numbers. This beautiful coin is very rare, and clearly underlines the neo-classical mood of the period by use of the allegory of UNA (Truth) and the lion.

denominations are included, together with the Maundy Set. The original case in which the proof coins were issued is unusual, in so much as it is spade-shaped.

The so-called Bonomi Pattern Crown Piece. Joseph Bonomi, an Egyptian traveller and antiquary, suggested and designed a crown piece as shown above to show how wear could be counteracted by having an incuse design. In 1893 specimens were issued for collectors by a friend of Bonomi's, and these occasionally feature in auction sales.

Soon after the Queen succeeded to the throne discussions arose as to whether Britain should have a decimal coinage, and after questions had been asked in Parliament two commissions were appointed to examine the possibilities. The result was the introduction of a coin as a tenth of a pound—a two-shilling piece. The motion introduced in Parliament, however, was for the pound to be split into hundredths of a pound; this was finally withdrawn by the proposer, Sir John Bowring, conditional to a tenth-of-a-pound-piece being circulated to test the public's reaction. Numerous patterns were struck, with names such as 'One decimal penny', 'Tenth of a penny', 'One hundred pence-one ducat', 'Half farthing-One Centime', '5 Francs International', etc.

It is interesting to recall the earlier attempts to 'introduce' decimal coinage. During Charles II's reign Sir William Petty, to 'keep all accompts in a way of Decimal Arithmetik', proposed that the penny should be split into five farthings (£1 to equal 1,200 farthings). Sir Christopher Wren agitated for an ounce of silver to be in one hundred

Smith's pattern Ten Cents. A private attempt to get decimalisation of the coinage accepted in 1846—1 cent = 1s. and 10c = 10s. illustrated here. Specimens are known in silver, copper, and white metal. (Peck 2078)

divisions, and Queen Anne, about 1710, supported Petty's idea of five farthings to the penny.

The Gothic Crown, issued in 1847 and 1853, has long had the reputation of being the world's most beautiful coin. Eight thousand coins were made, all of which are thought to have been in proof-state, i.e. carefully struck on polished blanks. Technically speaking, these unfrosted specimens are not called proofs. This term usually applied to the frosted early strikings, probably the first 200 to be made.

The Gothic Crown. Superlative is the only way to describe this magnificent design by William Wyon. The coin was a product of the Gothic revival, and as few as 8,000 were issued in 1847 and only 460 in 1853.

The edge legend on the 1847 coin reads as follows: DECUS*ET*TUTAMEN*ANNO*REGNO*UNDECIMO An ornament and a safeguard: (ISSUED IN) The eleventh year of our reign. On the 1853 coins issued in the specimen sets, this changes to 'SEPTIMO', i.e. the seventeenth year of Victoria's reign. A few 'Mules' exist (coins struck in error from the wrong dies), having the 1847 dated reverse with the SEPTIMO edge-legend; these are naturally very rare.

The florin of 1849 had Roman lettering, but in 1851 the beauty of this coin was much enhanced by the substitution of Gothic lettering for the obverse legend, together with

Punching out the Blank Coin

The Coining Press

The Rimming Machine

VICTORIAN MINTING METHODS

Obverse

Reverse

This well-worn 1868 half-crown prompted the TEMPLE organisation to carry out an investigation into unknown Victorian dates.

Gothic numerals for the date. An amusing story goes that when the 1849 florin was issued the 'D.G.' ('by the grace of God') was omitted from the legend. This was at the instigation of the Master of the Mint, who was a Roman Catholic and considered this entirely inappropriate. The coin was

The obverse of an 1878 half-crown, well circulated but still 'in collectable condition'.

known as the 'Godless Florin', and when the coin was re-designed in 1851 the 'D.G.' was replaced.

The issue of the 1853 proof set with the rare Gothic crown, half-crown, and all the other denominations, down to the half and quarter farthings, is probably the rarest of all the British specimen sets.

From 1851 to 1862 the half-crowns were discontinued in order that the public could become more acquainted with the florin. Proof half-crowns, however, dated 1851, 1853, 1862, and 1864 are known to exist. The half-crowns for ordinary issue were restored in 1874 by public request.

Until recently it was believed that a few collectors had made the discoveries of a lifetime, with unrecorded half-crowns made during the period 1851–73. In most cases the Royal Mint gave the owners letters saying the coins or coin in question were 'probably genuine' or 'we believe it to be a genuine half-crown'. Specimens turned up dated 1861, 1866, 1868, and 1871. From a detailed study of most of these coins and photographs, we at TEMPLE were able to prove conclusively that they were fakes.

There is a divergence of opinion as to the number of types of the Victorian young-head half-crown which exist. The text-book *The English Silver Coinage* published by Seaby describes six types: A1, A2, A2/3, A3, A4, A5; another distinct type has been recently added by splitting the last group into early A5 and late A5.

TEMPLE was able to establish that none of the odd date coins fitted into this grouping at the correct place, and thus with other design features proved the coins to be fakes.

A1		
A2		
A2/3	1839, 1840	
A3		
A4	1841–50	The 'unknown' coins should have been of either of these types. In fact, they conformed to the late A5 type.
Early A5	1874–79	
Late A5	1880–87	

These discoveries cleared up what had been an unsolved mystery and now prevent innocent collectors from parting with large sums of money for worthless coins.

From 1863 the Mint introduced numbered dies for many of the denominations, so that the life-span of any particular die could be ascertained. These numbered dies continued

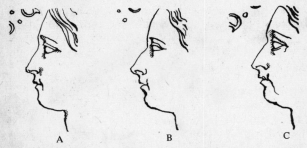

Bronze—portrait change. In an effort to show the fact that the queen had aged, the portrait on the bronze coinage was modified between 1860 and 1894/5.

    A 1860–73   B 1874–81   C 1881–94

until about 1874 on the sovereigns, where a die number can be seen on the reverse below the wreath. A number of sovereigns of this period, nevertheless, have no die number. The same situation applies to half-sovereigns, whose die numbers went on until 1880, but with the die number below the shield.

In addition to these, there are the sovereigns struck by Melbourne and Sydney Mints, which reveal a small M or S at the base of the shield on the reverse, or below the truncation of the neck on the obverse. On later types the M or S (or the letter P for Perth from 1899) can be found mid-way along the line that divides the date from the design.

Of the half-crowns, florins, shillings, and sixpences, some of the coins of similar periods have a die number, but others have none.

The reverses of the copper penny, halfpenny, and farthing copied the designs of the previous reign. Half farthings, too,

1   2

In 1881 the reverse of the bronze coinage was altered marginally and the shield was heraldically coloured, i.e. the colours were signified by ruled lines. It is worth noting that the lighthouse (probably Eddystone) had undergone minor modifications in design.

were struck in 1839, but until they were announced by proclamation as legal tender in 1842, they belonged to an issue for use in Ceylon only. In 1842 the design was changed, and they continued intermittently until 1856, the same year that groats ceased to be issued for the United Kingdom. The three larger copper denominations continued until 1859. The new bronze coins began in 1860 in pennies, halfpennies, and farthings with the legend transferred to the obverse and the date to the reverse.

A story, which gained considerable circulation regarding

the 1864 pennies, became so widespread, together with attempts to purchase them from the banks, that the Master of the Mint was compelled to make a public announcement denying it. The rumour was that gold had been accidentally mixed with the bronze, causing streaks of gold to be shown

1860 Bronze penny die varieties.
Reverse
1. Engraver's initials L. C. W. under shield. Beaded border.
2. Engraver's initials L. C. W. under Britannia's foot. Toothed border.
Obverse
3. L. C. Wyon on truncation. Beaded border.
4. L. C. Wyon on truncation. Toothed border.

on the surface of the coins. In fact, to give credence to this, streaks are occasionally seen; the trouble occurred in the physical mixing of bronze alloy.

When the 1887 gold and silver coins were struck with the much criticised Jubilee design of the Queen, which was intended to give her a more mature look (she was then sixty-eight years of age), the issue of bronze coins remained

Sixpence

Shilling

Crown

Three different examples of the Jubilee-head illustrating one fact even collectors miss, i.e. that although the bust is virtually the same in each case, the legend spacing alters significantly.

unchanged. The strange-looking crown 'perched' on her head could not possibly have 'stayed put', and does not appear to have been taken from a live sitting. At least Pistrucci's St. George and the Dragon on the reverse of the gold coins and crown compensated for the obverse in their respective cases, but the other denominations were sadly lacking. A new introduction to the normal issue was the double florin, or four-shilling piece, an outsize coin, which approximately represented the North American dollar. After four years, during which it proved unpopular, it ceased to be minted.

To celebrate the Queen's Golden Jubilee, the Royal Mint issued 797 proof sets comprising of gold (four coins) and silver (seven coins) only. There appear to be many more unofficial sets of uncirculated coin dated 1887 than there are proof sets. The 1887 sixpence achieved publicity because its reverse design changed three times in that year. First the Young Head design was 'run over' into the 1887 Jubilee Year; then with the Jubilee design on the obverse the

Double-Florin 1890.

'shield in garter' type was issued. This so closely resembled the half-sovereign that immediately gilded sixpences began to circulate as half-sovereigns. The Mint hurriedly withdrew the 'shield' coins and issued a coin with a new reverse decorated with the wreath design with a change in the type of crown above its denominational value.

Shillings showed the 'shield in garter' design, similar to the first Jubilee design sixpence. This was followed by a

An 1887 Shilling (reverse).

Familiar wreath—reverse composed of a laurel and oak-sprig—shown here on a 1890 sixpence.

second type, displaying the same reverse but with considerably larger bust of the Queen.

Perhaps the Jubilee-head groat or fourpenny piece of 1888 should be mentioned, as it is often documented as an English coin, although it was issued in British Guiana. This interesting little coin is now quite scarce, and in my opinion should figure in any complete type-set of the period.

1887 Crown Reverse. Strictly speaking, the 1887 was the first currency crown since 1845, assuming that the 1847 Gothic Issue was not released for circulation. Pistrucci's St. George well suited the crown, needing no fancy adornment and bearing no legend.

The Jubilee issue came to an end in 1892, except for the silver threepence, which continued into 1893. The number of this rare date that was struck with the Jubilee Head is unknown, as the Royal Mint kept no separate record of these, but merged the total in with the new old-head type.

The new issue of 1893/4 is known as the Old or Veiled Head Issue from a design by Sir Thomas Brock, the royal portrait receiving a better reception than its immediate predecessor. The artist showed a more natural portrait of the aged Queen, while the crown and veil looked as if they were part of a normal attire. The decorative jewellery, too, was more in keeping.

The changed design was accompanied by 773 proof sets of all the gold and silver coins (ten coins in all). An official silver proof set of six coins was also made available to the public.

Reverse of the 1878 sixpence reading DRITANNIAR instead of BRITANNIAR.

This final series continued unchanged until the death of the Queen in 1901, and although one or two individual coins are rare (e.g. the 1895 2-millimetre variety), the rest are all relatively common, except perhaps those in an uncirculated condition.

Throughout the long reign of Victoria the denominations of almost all issues have been marked by numerous minor varieties, particularly the period from 1838 to 1887, when individual dies varied from one another to a marked degree, creating many minor differences between coins that were intended to be identical. Space being limited, two excellent books worth looking at on the above subject are *English Copper, Tin, and Bronze Coins in the British Museum*, by

33

the late C. W. Peck and *The English Silver Coinage from 1649*, published by B. A. Seaby Ltd.

Both may be obtained at larger libraries, and will give the reader a real insight into the variety of coinage issued throughout Queen Victoria's lengthy reign.

CHAPTER II

EDWARD VII, 1902–10

Edward VII was born in Buckingham Palace on 9th November 1841. His official titles were 'King of Great Britain and of the Dominions beyond the Seas' and 'Emperor of India'. He was the elder son of Queen Victoria and Albert, Prince of Saxe-Coburg and Gotha.

Edward became Prince of Wales on 4th December 1841, and was privately tutored at Edinburgh University, where he studied chemistry and its industrial applications. He then went to Christ Church, Oxford, and Trinity College, Cambridge.

Postponed from 26th June 1902 because of the illness of the King, the Coronation took place at Westminster Abbey on 9th August 1902, and was proclaimed in India during a durbar at Delhi on New Year's Day, 1903.

At Windsor on 10th March 1863 the King married Alexandra of Denmark, daughter of King Christian IX; she quickly won the hearts of her British subjects. There were two sons, Albert Victor, who died in 1892, and George Frederick; there were three younger daughters—Louise, Victoria and Maud.

Edward proved to be a more able monarch than was expected, reviving court pageantry and enriching the glamour of the Crown through his own personality. He did much to improve international relations, particularly with France, becoming known as 'Edward the Peacemaker'.

His reign may be said to have been in two parts—1901–5, and 1905 until his death in 1910. The ministry during the earlier period was Unionist, with Balfour succeeding Salisbury as Prime Minister in July 1902. Edward's outlook was generally in sympathy with this latter government, by his own efforts contributing towards good relations in Europe (except perhaps with the German William II). In 1905 the Whigs came to power, and while the same foreign policy was adopted, social reforms and a quarrel with the House of Lords caused much bitterness. This was still in progress when the King died on 6th May 1910 from a bronchial weakness to which he had always been prone.

It was during his office as Prince of Wales that the estate at Sandringham was purchased on his behalf, it is said, from money saved during his minority, while his town residence became Marlborough House in London.

In 1894, as Prince of Wales, Edward officially opened Tower Bridge, and in the same year attended the Welsh Eisteddfod, being duly initiated. Two years later he became first Chancellor of the University College of Wales, being installed at Aberystwyth. For many years he had been a trustee of the British Museum and a member of the Standing Committee, with which he was very much concerned, attending with great regularity. He was a frequent visitor to the theatre and had a great interest in British sport, especially horse-racing.

Edward VII Coins

Edward VII's nine years of reign did not produce any really outstanding coinage apart from the florin. However, it is fair to say that almost all of the denominations of this single issue (1902–10) are much sought after, especially in top condition. The obverse design was by W. G. De Saulles, who produced an effigy of the King without any decoration whatsoever. An abbreviated form of the King's Latin style and title (proclaimed on 4th November 1901) was used for the surrounding legend. The only three reverses (including

De Saulle's masterful portrait of Edward VII, used from 1902 to 1910 on all the British regal coinage.

gold coins) to be changed from the last Victorian type were the half-crown, florin, and shilling.

The half-crown was modified by the shape of the shield being altered, the shilling was a copy of George IV's third-issue shilling by W. Wyon. Both these coins divided the legend between the obverse and reverse. The florin completely broke away from traditional designs, introducing the figure of Britannia holding a trident and resting against a shield while standing windswept on the prow of a ship. This was modelled for by the Chancellor of the Exchequer's daughter, Lady Susan Hicks-Beach. The 'long' Coronation proof or specimen set included the sovereign, half-sovereign, crown, and all the silver coins, including the Maundy Set. The 'short' set consisted of all the coins from the sovereign to the Maundy penny, omitting the five- and two-pound pieces. The surface of these has a 'matt' finish, giving a duller but iridescent appearance to a normal proof

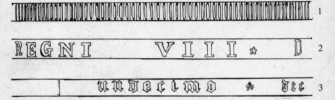

(1) A view of the modern reeded rim.
(2) Edge lettering normal style. (Eighth year of reign.)
(3) Gothic style. (Eleventh year of reign.)

issue, one of the few times in British numismatic history that this surface has been used for such a wide range of coinage.

Perhaps the most important introduction since the Frenchman Eloye Mestrelle's screw press was the two reducing machines brought from the Paris Mint in 1901 and 1902, producing master-dies for all coins and medals. These machines, no doubt to the sorrow of many numismatists, eliminated the level of variation in individual dies, while at the same time reproducing faithfully designs from crown to the Maundy penny.

The reverse of a 1902 ⅓ farthing, issued for use in Malta.

Medal—issued to commemorate Victoria's Diamond Jubilee, showing four generations of the monarchy, Victoria, Edward VII, George V, and Edward VIII.

When the very small mintage figures of this reign are considered it is not surprising that the collector demand is coupled with a great shortage of quality specimens. Only four times did the annual coinage issue of any denomination exceed double figures in millions. Undoubtedly the rarest coin of this series is the 1905 half-crown (mintage figure 166,008), which is rarely seen today in any condition. There are a number of low mintages for this reign, however, commanding considerably higher prices than one might

The superlative standing Britannia as depicted on the florins of Edward VII. Shown here the rare 1905 date.

expect. These are the crowns of 1902 (25,602), half-crowns of 1903 (274,840) and 1904 (709,652), florins of 1905 (1,187,596), and shillings of 1905 (488,390). While mintage figures can be a guide, they are not always a true indication of scarcity, as numbers of coins about this period were dispatched to countries in the British Empire to supply the needs of developing communities. It has been frequently observed that coins circulated in small communities are finally returned to the Royal Mint in a far more worn condition than those from London. Even in remoter provincial areas of Britain, where coins remain in a tighter circulating area, banks have reported that silver coins returned in £100 bags are lighter in weight than from areas in more direct communication with the capital.

While discussing wear on Edward's coins, it is worth noting the big disadvantage of the new florin. To put it simply, the date wore off after a short circulation, being one of the highest spots on the entire coin. This dubious attribute pushes up the value of perfect specimens, since there is a high rejection rate of worn coins among collectors.

CHAPTER III

GEORGE V, 1911–1936

George V was born at Marlborough House, 3rd June 1865, son of Edward VII, who at that time was still Prince of Wales.

In 1877 both George and his elder brother Albert entered the Royal Navy, and in 1880 made a world tour in H.M.S. Bacchante, from which the letters, diaries, and note-books of the princes were published under the title of *The Cruise of H.M.S. Bacchante*. At the end of the tour the brothers separated, with George remaining in the Navy. He was promoted to Sub-Lieutenant, H.M.S. *Canada* on the North American and West Indies station. After passing through the R.N. college at Greenwich he was promoted to Lieutenant in 1885, and served successively in H.M.S. *Thunderer, Dreadnought, Alexandra*, and *Northumberland*. He was promoted in 1891 to Commander, in 1893 to Captain, in 1901 to Rear-Admiral, and in 1903 to Vice-Admiral. He had a natural aptitude for seamanship, and loved the life. He was a frequent and familiar figure at Cowes, and the yacht *Britannia* would regularly be seen racing with the prince in command. His Naval career ended, however, in 1892 when his elder brother died, necessitating Prince George to take over the affairs of state, about which he knew very little.

His upbringing was bound by a tradition which showed signs of Victorian influence. He had a great admiration for his father Edward, although he was unlike him in many characteristics. Whereas Edward was gay and vivacious and loved lively company, George was quiet, less emotional, and more like the traditional squire who loved country life.

On 6th July 1893 he married the Princess Victoria Mary of Teck. They had six children, Edward (later Edward VIII), Albert (later George VI), Mary, Henry, George, and John.

In March 1901 the Prince and Princess sailed in the *Ophir* on a world cruise. They landed at Melbourne in May 1901, where the Prince opened the first Parliament of the Commonwealth. This was followed by a visit to New Zealand, returning via South Africa and Canada.

At his Coronation in Westminster Abbey on 22nd June 1911 the brilliance of the ceremony surprised those who knew him, but it soon became apparent that in spite of his previously simple life he intended to outshine even the Edwardian Court where public functions were concerned. This policy was further developed with the weddings of Princess Mary in 1922, the Duke of York (George VI) in 1923, and the Duke of Kent (Prince George) in 1934, all at Westminster Abbey. On 17th July 1917 the King proclaimed the abandonment of all German titles held by the Royal family, and announced that the Royal house of Great Britain and Ireland would in future be known as the House of Windsor.

Apart from their numerous war-time visits to the French and Belgian Fronts, where their presence was to have good effect on morale, the fine record of the King and Queen of visiting places is noteworthy. At the end of the war, immediately after the Armistice in 1918, they visited consecutively many areas of London, where they received tremendous ovations. On 21st–22nd June 1921 they visited Belfast, where the King inaugurated the new Parliament of Northern Ireland. Many consider that his advocation of forbearance and forgiveness, to the people of Ireland as a whole contributed largely in bringing about a new era of peace. Following later visits to Belgium and Italy in 1922 and 1923, they performed many ceremonies at home, including the great British Empire Exhibition at Wembley in 1924, the dedication of Liverpool Cathedral, and the opening of the Mersey Tunnel. In 1932 the King gave the first Royal Christmas message to the Commonwealth, a practice continued by George VI and Elizabeth II. Further events of great importance were the first Labour Government in 1924, the General Strike in 1926, the economic crisis of 1931, and an introduction of a new Indian constitution.

The notable event of the Silver Jubilee in 1935 was marked by the tremendous enthusiasm of the people, revealing the great affection which the King and Queen had so justly earned.

His insistence to stay in Great Britain throughout the 1935–36 winter in spite of a medical warning was one example of his generous self-sacrificing nature. He took a chill and died on 20th January 1936.

King George's reign, except for brief periods, was turbulent and troubled. There was labour unrest, suffragette agitation, and Irish disturbances, followed by the First World War with its terrible death toll.

King George himself was an ardent stamp collector, and his collection has been described as the most complete in the world.

George V Coins

The same denominations of Edward VII's reign, dated 1911, continued when George V ascended the throne, but

1910 pattern George V crown. This St. George and dragon reverse by A. G. Wyon (second type) is rarely seen by collectors, as only ten were struck.

the reverse of the florin was changed in favour of a design by the Royal Mint, obviously based on the famous Petition Crown of Thomas Simon. While this design does not achieve the classic finish of Simon's, it is a big improvement on the Victorian double florin and florin, which also copied the Simon design. Writer Gertrude Rawlings, in her useful book on the English coinage, ridicules the four-shilling piece as 'radiating kitchen-pokers and tea-trays'.

The other coin to have a new reverse design was the sixpence, on which a lion is shown above the crown. In 1911 three types of proof sets for collectors were issued—the all-silver set (including the four Maundy coins), a similar set plus the sovereign and half-sovereign, and thirdly, a set similar to the second plus the five- and two-pound pieces.

Pattern four shillings 1911 by Huth. The double florin was never a popular coin, and these irrelevant patterns could never really have had very much success as coins.

A full complement of gold, silver, and bronze coins was issued until the First World War broke out in 1914. The Government immediately put into motion the production of paper currency. Notes to the values of £1 and 10s. were issued to replace gold, and became legal tender anywhere in the United Kingdom. This issue proved a great success, as the public accepted it, surrendering their sovereigns and half sovereigns to the banks, who, in turn, surrendered them to the Bank of England. Gold sovereigns quickly disappeared from circulation. In 1915 the production of half-sovereigns at the Royal Mint completely ceased, while sovereigns virtually ended in the same year; however, small quantities continued in 1916 and 1917 for special purposes. When the war ended sovereigns, with a 1925 date on them, continued to be issued in small quantities for a number of years after this date. It is surprising, in view of the quantity handed in to the Bank of England, how many sovereigns have, after fifty years, remained in such excellent condition. No doubt

A 1911 florin. The reverse has allusions to the Jubilee florin/double florin design once described as resembling tea-trays and pokers.

the bulk of them have been hidden away in various homes and have been brought to light by the second- and third-generation owners, in whom the original sentimental attachments no longer exist. The price of world silver had risen to such a proportion that it was an embarrassment to the Treasury, a silver half-crown being worth 3s. 4d. As a result, the silver coinage, which had contained 92·5% silver in 1919 and earlier issues, was reduced to 50% silver in the 1920 issue, eliminating illegal melting down. It is interesting to note that some of the 1920 sixpences were struck in

92.5% silver. This fact generally escapes the attention of collectors and dealers alike. Presumably this is caused by the uncertainty of identification between the two types. There should be, however, little doubt of this when one good specimen of each type is compared with the other. The 92.5%'s are outstandingly 'whiter' in appearance than that of the commoner issue. In 1918/19 there was a vast increase in the demand for coinage throughout the world. Due to this, the Royal Mint was obliged to contract out much of the United Kingdom bronze coins, which had been produced in certain past years by Heaton and Son of Birmingham. The earlier years, when Heatons undertook this work, were in 1874–76, 1881, 1882 for both pennies and halfpennies, and in 1881 and 1882 for farthings. Heaton's mint mark on these is a very small 'H' beneath the date. In 1912, 1918, and 1919 they again produced pennies for the Royal Mint, but their mint mark on these were to the left of the date. Another firm was also given a contract to produce pennies in these last two years. They were the Kings Norton Metal Company of Birmingham, with their mint mark 'KN' placed also to the left of the date. A common but erroneous belief with the public and uninformed collectors is that these coins are of great value. While it is true that they command a premium among collectors and are scarcer than the Royal Mint issues (with no mint mark), the increased value is very small by comparison. It is true, of course, that brilliant uncirculated 'H's' and 'KN's' are very rare and command a considerable sum.

The 'fifty-fifty' silver created considerable problems for the Royal Mint, as the copper (40%) and the nickel (10%)

A pattern 1925 threepence with a scalloped edge. This may well have been a fore-runner of the nickel-brass threepence first issued in 1937.

A pattern 1925 shilling in nickel, designed by Kruger Gray.

A pattern 1925 threepence in nickel with the acorn reverse not instituted until 1927.

mixed badly in the new silver coinage, and the 1920 and 1921 coins revealed the copper in patches on the coin surface. The fault was partially overcome in the following year

The obverse of a (machine-made forgery) 1920 half-crown—one of the few ways of telling this coin is the exaggerated downstroke of the 'D' of DEI. *Note:* This was the year when the change in the silver content occurred, from 0·925 to 0·500 fine.

by omitting the nickel entirely and increasing the copper to 50%. The problem was finally overcome by using 40% copper, 5% nickel, and 5% zinc. At this time there began a definite move by the Royal Mint to give every opportunity for improvement in the cultivation of numismatic art. Leading artists and connoisseurs formed a committee in 1923 to advise the Mint on the designs of coins. The general trend set by this committee was clearly towards innovations and new designs. Results were soon obtained in 1927–36 issue, a particularly fine set of coins, which included the first

Reverse of a (machine-made forgery) 1920 half-crown.

crown issued since Edward VII's coronation. This fully justified the introduction of the new committee and also revealed, by the greatly improved surface lustre of the coins, that the Mint had satisfactorily overcome their problem of mixing the metals. This issue did not begin until 1928, as the 1927 coins were proof coins only. The coins were

CANADIAN
MINT-MARK.

1918 S.P

1918 C SOVEREIGN.

This diagram shows how to distinguish the origin of a sovereign showing a Canadian 'C' mint mark. Other mint marks include 'M' for Melbourne, 'P' for Perth, 'S' for Sydney, and 'SA' for Pretoria—South African Mints.

received by the public with considerable favour after the discoloured and easily worn second issue of 1920–26.

The new crown, known as the 'Wreath Crown', because of its reverse design, is particularly worthy of a more detailed description. Its existence is in no small measure due to the efforts of Sir Charles Oman, then a Member of

The wreath crown issued between 1927 and 1934–36.

The modernistic St. George and the dragon reverse of the 1935 crown, which looks better from a line drawing than the coin itself.

Parliament for Oxford University and President of the Royal Numismatic Society. The small numbers for each year of issue emphasise the fact that they were for collectors only, and not for circulation. The total number of crowns for the eight years of issue was only 50,893 (excluding the 1935 coins). It is not surprising, therefore, bearing in mind the world-wide collector demand for crown-size coins, that

↖ Altered
date

The much publicised 1933 penny—or is it? In fact, this coin has been altered and was originally dated 1935 or 1936. They are quite common, and tricksters have been known to pass them off on to innocent collectors.

their values are unusually high. The 1934 year has the lowest mintage of only 932 coins, while the highest is that of 1927, when all but thirty crowns were included in the officially issued proof sets, reaching a total of 15,000.

When the King and Queen reached their Silver Jubilee in 1935 the issue of the Wreath Crown was shelved and the Commemorative Jubilee Crown was issued instead. The reverse was by Percy Metcalfe, who reproduced a modern version of Pistrucci's 'St. George and the Dragon', a design

which was much criticised. The incuse edge lettering reads
DECUS ET TUTAMEN ANNO REGNI XXV to record the Silver
Jubilee. There are four interesting varieties, three of which
are extremely rare. The first is identical to the normal issue
(0·500 silver), but in 92·5 silver with the edge lettering
raised. The second is indistinguishable from the normal
issue, but is of 92·5 silver with an incuse edge-legend.
Identification presents something of a problem, as there is

A further example of a Lavrillier 1933 pattern penny, which is very
scarce.

very little difference in colour between this crown and the
normal issue. A third type is of the raised-lettering variety,
in gold; however, only twenty-five of these are in existence.
The final and best-known type is the 'Error-edge' variety,
which reads DECUS ANNO REGNI ET TUTAMEN XXV instead of
as above.

Throughout George V's coinage the portrait was
designed by Sir Bertram Mackennal. His initials, B.M.,
appear on the truncation of the bust. In 1926, however, the
effigy of the King was slightly reduced and the B.M. initials

moved a little to the rear of the truncation, and a new beaded border added. This is known as the modified effigy (abbreviation M.E.), and is more sought after than the normal issue.

From 1927 the reverses were designed by Kruger Gray, but the earlier issues were mostly designs readjusted by the Mint.

Certain years of this period (excluding the 1927 proof sets) have denominations with low mintages. These automatically attract attention because of their scarcity and are shown below with the average annual mintage for the nine-year period.

Denomination	Year of issue	Number issued	Annual averaged
Half-crowns	1930	809,051	8,110,959
Florins	1932	717,041	7,403,855
Shillings	1930	3,137,092	10,947,007
Threepence	1928	1,302,106	4,223,511
	1930	1,319,412	,,

The death of George V on 20th January 1936, the abdication of his eldest son Edward VIII on 11th December 1936, followed by the succession of George VI, meant that technically there were three Kings in the same year. The coinage of 1936 displaying George V's effigy is sometimes credited to Edward VIII on the grounds that the coinage was struck during the latter's reign.

CHAPTER IV

EDWARD VIII, 1936

Edward VIII was born on 23rd June 1894 at White Lodge, Richmond Park.

From 1902 until 1914 he was accompanied by his tutor, H. P. Hansell, to various places of education. During the next five years he was educated with a view to joining the Navy, and in 1907–9 he went to Osborne, a preparatory Naval College in the Isle of Wight, followed by training at R.N. College, Dartmouth.

On his sixteenth birthday he was created Prince of Wales and invested three weeks later by the King at Caernarvon Castle. Edward was the first English Prince of Wales to address the Welsh people in their own language, a precedent followed by Prince Charles.

In 1912 Edward entered Magdalen College, Oxford, where he was, in the main, permitted to be just another undergraduate, unlike previous sheltered Royal persons, and made many friends there. There is one amusing story which typifies his general attitude to his fellow men and those in lower walks of life. After a considerable but inconclusive argument with an extreme socialist fellow student he won this student over to his way of thinking (or at least showed his sense of humour) by singing 'The Red Flag' to an accompaniment on his own banjo!

The Prince's university career, however, ended abruptly when the First World War broke out in 1914. Edward was most rebellious against many of the restrictions imposed upon him as a soldier; obviously those answerable for the heir to the throne would not take the responsibility of allowing him in the firing line. His natural desire was to share equal comradeship with those of lower rank than himself.

He became the first Chairman of the newly formed committee relating to the Naval and Military Pensions Act in 1916. Subsequently, he spent a very active time in the Army abroad, serving in Egypt with the Expeditionary Force and in Italy and France. After the Italian defeat at Caporetto in October 1917 he again returned to Italy, remaining there until nearly the end of the war.

Edward's early life was full of great promise and he enjoyed immense popularity both in Great Britain and in all the countries he visited. From any standard, he was widely travelled, having visited many parts of the world between the years 1919 and 1925 in the capacity of Ambassador.

He displayed great interest in social problems and on a number of occasions made personal contact with the people suffering in the aftermath of war. Frequently the Prince's habit of mixing with the crowd, often with no certainty as to how it would react, caused considerable anxiety to those who were responsible for his safety.

During his visit to Nigeria he took part in a durbar with 20,000 horsemen led by their Moslem chieftains; it was said to have been an incredibly colourful sight. On this same tour, when he reached Cape Town, he greatly pleased the Dutch with his first speech by including a few Afrikaan sentences. In 1931 Edward purchased Fort Belvedere and altered it to his requirements as a country house. This residence, within the confines of Windsor Great Park, had been built in the mid-eighteenth century by the Duke of Cumberland.

As an uncrowned monarch with so much promise, it was indeed tragic that his short reign was so soon ended by his decision to abdicate. The few acts he performed during his reign and the always joyful reception he received from the people underlined the nation's loss.

His special visits to distressed areas of chronic unemployment showed his deep concern with these problems. The King inspected the housing progress in the slum areas of Glasgow and also visited the new liner *Queen Mary*, and he visited South Wales, an area of acute unemployment. His outspoken comments championed the cause of those pressing for greater action. He was not backward in taking an active part in matters of industry.

The events leading to the King's abdication as an uncrowned monarch on 11th December 1936 were caused by Parliament and the Church finding the King's proposed marriage unacceptable to the nation. Finally, the choice Edward had was between his marriage to Mrs. Simpson and the Crown. The King, determined to marry the woman of his choice, took the course he felt was correct and abdicated. When the public became fully aware of the situation they were deeply moved, and there was a great desire for him to remain King, a sentiment to be expected about a man who had won so much respect and popularity with the people.

Immediately following his abdication he was created Duke of Windsor by his brother George VI, who succeeded him. On 3rd June 1937 he married Mrs. Simpson at the Chateau de Conde, France, and has resided in that country since that time.

Edward VIII Coins

No coins bearing Edward's portrait were issued for general circulation in Britain although issues were made in certain Colonial countries. Unofficial crowns struck in both gold and silver from four different countries, America, Bermuda, Ceylon and Australia, are known to exist. Of the American issue 25 were struck in gold and 50 in silver, with the respective prices of £80 and £40. These are occasionally auctioned in various parts of the world, and while there must be an interest in them, their legality remains in doubt. The obverse of the gold coin shows the bareheaded Edward VIII facing left with the inscription EDWARD VIII KING & EMPEROR; the reverse displays St. George and the Dragon also turning to the left with the date beneath. The silver crown is similar, but the reverse faces to the right.

Cupro-nickel coins with the name EDWARD VIII in the legend of the one penny, halfpenny, and one-tenth penny, all dated 1936, were issued for British West Africa. Similarly, two bronze coins with the name EDWARD VIII in the legend were issued with values of 10 and 5 cents for East Africa.

His reign was obviously too short to produce a coinage, although a full complement of denominations, as in George

V's reign, had been struck at the Royal Mint before his abdication. Included in this issue was a completely new type of coin with an entirely new reverse design for British coins, the now popular dodecagonal nickel-brass threepenny piece displaying the thrift plant. As this coin was an entirely new shape, twelve sided, a number were loaned to manufacturers of slot machines and meters for testing, but not all the

The Edward VIII 1937 nickel-brass threepence. This much publicised piece was the only British coin ever to have borne the portrait of Edward VIII, who abdicated in favour of his brother George VI.

coins were returned after use. These therefore, must be the threepenny pieces which have escaped into collectors' hands, to which must be added a few smuggled out of the Royal Mint. A uniface (one-sided) pattern florin was recently discovered, with a reverse similar to that used for George VI. Pattern bronze coins of Edward VIII also exist in the British Museum.

When Edward abdicated on 11th December 1936 all his coinage was placed in the 'melting pot' without any being issued, except those which were illegally retained. The dies were also destroyed at the same time.

CHAPTER V

GEORGE VI, 1937–52

George VI was born at York Cottage, Sandringham, on 14th December 1895. He was also known as Prince Albert—his first Christian name. When old enough, he followed the traditional training path in the Royal Navy, via Osborne in the Isle of Wight and then on to Dartmouth, where he received his Commission. In 1916 he joined the Grand Fleet as a Sub-Lieutenant and fought in the Battle of Jutland. He was also a Naval cadet at the Royal Air Force establishment at Cranwell and in October 1918 served on the Western Front. When peacetime came, he spent several terms at Trinity College, Cambridge.

George was created Duke of York, Baron of Killarney, Earl of Inverness on 3rd June 1920 and married Lady Elizabeth Bowes Lyons on 26th April 1923. Their two children were our present Queen, Elizabeth (born 21st April 1926) and her younger sister Margaret (born 21st August 1930).

As Duke of York he was never expected to rule the country and, like his father before him, was never educated with this in mind. He was a deeply sincere man, handicapped by an impediment in his speech, which caused him to be shy and retiring. Nor did he possess the talents that made Edward his brother so popular as Prince of Wales. Nevertheless, to his great credit, he overcame these obstacles and endeared himself to the nation by his kindness and sincerity, aided so nobly by his devoted Queen.

Although he had not experienced much travelling within the Empire, he had gained considerable knowledge through his Naval training, and it was an event of great importance when he and the Duchess sailed to Australia in 1927, to open the Australian Parliament at Canberra.

On the abdication of his brother Edward VIII on 11th December 1936 he became King George VI. Their Majesties were crowned on 12th May 1937. Throughout the following three summers they paid visits to Ulster, France, Canada, and the United States, in that order. It was during the Second World War that the King and Queen earned the popularity and gratitude of the people by their own seemingly inexhaustible energy in visiting hospitals, service units, dockyards, munitions factories, bombed areas, etc., as well as making trips overseas to the areas of fighting.

After the war the King visited Eisenhower's headquarters and also the newly liberated Channel Isles. This was followed by the King taking the salute of the Victory Parade in the Mall on 5th June 1946. In 1947 their Majesties and the two Princesses sailed in the *Vanguard* to South Africa.

It was in this year that fundamental changes took place in the Commonwealth. The two self-governing states of India and Pakistan were created, with the King no longer holding the title of Emperor.

A tour in 1949, similar to the South African one, was also planned for Australia and New Zealand, but this was cancelled owing to the King's illness. His sudden death at Sandringham on 6th February 1952 came as a shock to the nation, who had little idea that he had fought against ill-health for the greater part of his life.

George VI Coins

George VI became King only 2½ years before the out-break of the Second European World War, a tragedy which

The armorial reverse of a 1937 crown.

had a considerable effect on the coinage during and after the war years. In 1937 a full complement of coinage was issued, with denominations as in the previous reign, together with two completely new innovations. The first of these was

66

the nickel-brass, twelve-sided threepence, with the thrift plant on the reverse—a coin which, as described earlier, had been intended to replace the little silver threepenny piece in Edward VIII's reign. Its metal content was 79%

This is not a coin but an impression from a trial-die used by the Royal Mint sometimes when testing new alloys. Contrary to normal opinion, the figure represents a soldier striking coins and *not* Britannia.

copper, 20% zinc, and 1% nickel. The public did not take to it immediately, and after the first year the banks reported that they had unwanted accumulations of it in their safes. In addition, the silver threepenny piece was still very popular in Scotland and was in considerable demand. This caused the Royal Mint to continue production of both types until 1941. It was decided, however, to continue a small silver issue dated 1942 for the West Indies, where they were still in common use. These coins continued to be made in 1943 and 1944, with both issues dated accordingly. In the jargon of the coin dealers this coin was known as a 'joey', a name used derogatively and derived from a foreshortening of Joseph Chamberlain's name. A 1945 silver threepenny was also intended, but the Royal Mint were given instructions to melt down the whole of this batch, together with the unissued remainder of the 1944. The Royal Mint estimate that one-third of the 1944 coins were destroyed, alongside the total 1945's. It is therefore correct to assume that the 1944 silver threepenny issue is about $1\frac{1}{3}$ million, not 'just over 2 million', as quoted in most coin guides. It is debatable whether the 1942/3/4 silver threepenny issue may be

1937 silver threepence reverse, with the shield of St. George on a Tudor rose dividing the date. This coin was doomed with the introduction of its brass equivalent.

classed as an English coin or whether it should belong to the West Indies, similar to the 1888 British groat, issued for Colonial use.

The second innovation of interest was the additional one-shilling coin with a reverse based on an old Scottish design. This was a compliment to the new Queen's Scottish ancestry, her present title being the Queen Mother. The 1937 crown was completely redesigned with a new reverse—the Royal Arms with supporters and a surrounding legend. Both the half-crown and English shilling reverses were modified, while those of the florin, sixpence, and silver threepence were completely redesigned. The half-crown was

Notice →
the 'Dot'

The 1946 'Dot' variety penny. One of the many new varieties recently discovered.

an adaptation of Kruger Gray's design for the previous reign by T. H. Paget, while Kruger Gray was responsible for the remaining silver coin reverses. The portrait on the obverses was by Paget.

With the fluctuating price of silver in the world market, it was decided in 1946 that silver metal should be entirely omitted from the coinage, to be substituted by a mixture of copper and nickel on 1st January 1947. [With the numerous

The 1937 florin reverse, which gives the appearance of being very cluttered.

lessons in the past when the silver coins became of greater value than their metal content—the most recent example was in 1920, when a silver half-crown became worth 3s. 4d.—it was a wise decision, as the extremely high price of silver in the late sixties has shown.] The composition of the cupro-nickel coinage was 75% copper and 25% nickel, giving a much harder and more durable coin than the 50% silver content. The edge graining on these coins was much finer than on the coins they superseded, and the two types may be easily separated by their edges. The Maundy coins, however, remained silver; in fact, their silver content was raised from the 50% it had been reduced to in 1920 to 92·5%, as it had been in 1919 and before. The use of cupro-nickel metal in coinage was not new to the Royal Mint, as in 1869 they had produced the penny and halfpenny for Jamaica, and Belgium struck their 5 and 10 centimes that same year. Both the Americans and the Swiss had experimented with a copper—nickel mixture for coins as early as 1857. It is said that this search for new combinations was a direct result of a copper coins shortage in France after the French Revolution. While the revolution was at its peak, the mob, bent on destruction, tore down even the church bells. When peace was finally restored, the French Mint, in an effort to find a use for these broken bells, experimented with the metal in them. By melting them down, they were able to produce a hard and serviceable coin. Finally, as the majority of bells had been re-utilised, copper was mixed in with the 'bell metal'. Coins realised in this metal became known as 'sous des clochers' (belfry halfpennies). This alloy was made legal in France; other countries followed their lead.

India and Pakistan divided in 1947, each becoming a separate independent republic within the Commonwealth. This had a significant effect on the British coinage, causing the legend around the coins to be altered by omitting the abbreviated IND. IMP. (short for INDIAE IMPERATOR) from all the coins bearing the date 1949 and after.

During the war years it appeared that quantities of newly minted pennies were being withheld from normal circulation. The official reason given for this was that the brightly coloured coins were being hoarded by collectors, greedy for glitter. To counteract this, the Mint artificially toned down the surface brilliance by a chemical treatment using hyposulphite. From 1947 pennies were issued with the normal lustre, as it was assumed that hoarding by the public had been discontinued. The penny reverse from 1937 showed a slight modification of Britannia and a lighthouse in the background, said to have been taken from the Eddystone light-

The GRI monogram from the first type of George VI sixpences, representing the title GEORGIUS REX IMPERATOR, which was altered in 1947, when the title Emperor of India was dropped.

house. The halfpenny had a completely new reverse, as did the farthing, the former displaying a sailing ship reputed to be Drake's *Golden Hind*—the first English ship to sail around the world—and the latter displaying the smallest of the birds of Great Britain—the Wren.

Due to the Japanese invasion, tin supplies from Malaya ceased. This metal shortage resulted in the bronze coinage from 1942 being made with only $\frac{1}{2}\%$ tin, whereas previously the amount had been 3%.

In 1950 the Royal Mint quite surprisingly issued a proof set of coins with all denominations except a crown: surprising, because 'The Mid-Century Set', as it was called, hardly justified a special issue of coins. In the next year another proof set was issued. This included the crown piece, noteworthy as it again reintroduced Pistrucci's famous St. George and the Dragon. The production of the larger coin in cupro-nickel represented a triumph for the Royal Mint,

Pistrucci's St. George was so good that it was chosen as the reverse for the 1951 Festival of Britain Commemorative crown.

as harder metal over a larger surface presented a possible problem; this was overcome: the result, the well-struck 1951 Festival of Britain Crown. All these were issued as proof specimens, mostly in small individual boxes; the remainder was issued in proof sets of 5s. to a $\frac{1}{4}d$. Around the coin edge is the inscription MDCCCLI CIVIUM INDUSTRIA FLORET CIVITAS MCMLI (1851. By the Industry of its people the State flourishes. 1951). Twenty thousand of these sets were issued.

To show the tremendous rise in the demand for coins by collectors, it is interesting to recall that the issue price of the 1950 and 1951 proof sets by the Royal Mint were 20s. and 25s. respectively.

In the year after the Festival of Britain (February 1952) the King died. Coins programmed at the Royal Mint for that year were abandoned, although 1952 sixpences totalling $1\frac{1}{3}$ millions, already arranged to supply the West Indies, were despatched. To be consistent with earlier Victorian issues to the colonies, we should strictly place the 1952 sixpence as a West Indies issue. One 'genuine' 1952 half-crown is known to exist, and was probably a trial piece.

CHAPTER VI

ELIZABETH II, 1953–

Elizabeth II was born on 21st April 1926, in Bruton Street, London, W.1, the home of her maternal grandparents, the Earl and Countess of Strathmore. She was the elder daughter of the Duke and Duchess of York (later George VI and Queen Elizabeth). The Duke was the second son of George V.

Her education was private, arranged by her mother (now Elizabeth the Queen Mother), who entrusted both Elizabeth and her sister Margaret to a governess. Elizabeth's first public contact was at the age of 14, when she broadcast to the children of the Empire who were evacuated from their homes. During the early part of the Second World War she and her sister were at Balmoral, while during the latter part of the war they lived at the Royal Lodge, Windsor.

The young Princess made her first public appearance in the summer of 1944, when she met the governors of the Queen Elizabeth Hospital for Children. After joining the A.T.S. in 1945 as a driver at her own request (after some official opposition) she carried out an increasing number of public engagements. One outstanding occasion was in 1947 at the age of 21, when she visited South Africa with the King and Queen; here she broadcast to the Commonwealth, underlining her promise of devotion to 'the service of our great imperial family' and the motto (which is the personal emblem of the Prince of Wales)—'I serve' (Ich Dien). In June of the same year her engagement to Lt. Philip Mountbatten, R.N. (formerly Prince Philip of Greece and

An equestrian portrait of the Queen in her role as Colonel in Chief of the Grenadier Guards was chosen as the obverse theme for the 1953 Coronation Crown.

Denmark) was announced. The marriage took place at Westminster Abbey on 20th November 1947, Prince Philip having been created Duke of Edinburgh before the ceremony. Charles (now Prince of Wales and heir apparent) was born on 14th November 1948 at Buckingham Palace, followed by Princess Anne (born 1950), Prince Andrew (born

1960), and Prince Edward (born 1964).

After the serious operation on her father, the King, she went with Prince Philip on 7th October 1951 on a highly successful tour of Canada, also visiting Washington in the United States. The following year they again began another Commonwealth tour. It was at this time, in Kenya, that news came of the death of the King in February 1952, and the tour was abandoned.

The Coronation of the Queen took place in Westminster Abbey on 2nd June 1953. In November they began another Commonwealth tour, returning to England in May 1954. This tour included visits to Australia, New Zealand (from where the Queen delivered her Christmas broadcast to the Commonwealth peoples), Fiji, Uganda, Malta, and Gibraltar.

From this time the Queen and Prince Philip continued a very crowded programme of public engagements at home and abroad, which included France, the United States, Canada, Ethiopia, India, and the German Federal Republic.

In 1957 the Queen made history by appearing and making a speech on television for the first time.

Since the Queen's reign began many changes in traditional customs have taken place with the object of modernising the monarchy, reducing the formal occasions to those really needed, substituting informality whenever possible. This approach has had the desirable effect of removing much of the pressure and strain that would otherwise be imposed upon the Queen. Simplified communications and mass media, television and cinema news, have made her and the Royal Family popular figures to people all over the world.

Queen Elizabeth's ascent to the throne required the production of a completely new coinage. With this objective, the Royal Mint Advisory Committee, under the presidency of the Duke of Edinburgh, immediately set to work inviting artists to submit designs. Their requirements were for the head of the Queen to be in profile, and following tradition, facing to the right. The committee, however, stated that there was a preference for a head-and-shoulders portrait.

It is a point of interest that on our coinage each succeeding monarch has faced in the opposite direction to his or her immediate predecessor; however, George V, Edward VIII (i.e. the rare nickel brass 3d. piece), and George VI all faced left. Edward VIII especially requested his profile to face left, but as no coins of his were officially issued it is assumed that he would have faced right, and the continuity of the custom continued.

The acceptance of Gilbert Ledward's obverse design for the crown piece was a complete break with modern tradition, the last coin to exhibit a monarch on horseback was minted during Charles I's reign (1625–49).

Elizabeth II Coins

This portrait of the Queen was taken from a well-known photograph of Her Majesty as Colonel-in-Chief, Grenadier Guards, at the Trooping of the Colour. The reverse bears an arresting design by E. G. Fuller and Cecil Thomas, and while it carries the four quarterings of the Royal Arms in four separate shields, the traditional double rose, thistle, shamrock, and leek, with the date at the base, it does not appear to be overcrowded. The inscription on the edge,

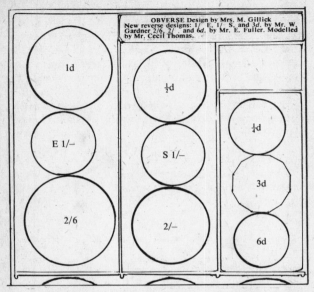

OBVERSE Design by Mrs. M. Gillick.
New reverse designs: 1/- E, 1/- S, and 3d. by Mr. W. Gardner 2/6, 2/- and 6d. by Mr. E. Fuller. Modelled by Mr. Cecil Thomas.

1d

½d

¼d

E 1/-

S 1/-

3d

2/6

2/-

6d

Illustrated here is the layout of the 1953 'plastic set' of coins issued to the general public by banks in the Coronation year. This diagram shows the average layout in which the coins were presented.

'Faith and Truth I will bear unto you', comes from the Oath of Homage in the Coronation Service.

The Queen's bust on the obverse of all the remaining coins is the work of Mary Gillick. One immediate impression of this design is that the effigy of the Queen does not fill the required space.

A number of artists were invited to submit designs for the reverse, the task of selection being left to the Royal Mint Advisory Committee. From a short list of seventeen the work of E. G. Fuller and W. Gardner was chosen, the former designing the half-crown, florin, and sixpence; the English and Scottish shilling and threepence designed by the latter.

The half-crown displays the shield of the Royal Arms, surmounted by a crown with the shield dividing the letters

The portcullis figured on the reverse of Elizabeth II's brass threepence, designed by William Gardner and issued from 1953 to 1967. The treatment of this design is masterful and puts our present decimal coins to shame.

E.R. The florin, in its central inner circle, shows the double rose surrounded by thistles, shamrocks, and leeks. The English shilling has a centrally placed shield containing the three leopards from the Royal Arms, surmounted by the crown, while the Scottish shilling is similar except that the shield contains a lion rampant. The sixpence has a floral reverse, showing the interlaced emblems of the rose, thistle, shamrock, and leek. In each case the legend FID. DEF. is written above with the amount in words below, followed by the date 1953. The threepence displays an adaptation of Henry VII's badge—a portcullis with chains ensigned, and a royal coronet above. Of the bronze coins issued, only half-pennies and farthings were for general circulation, as the penny was intended to be issued only as part of the 1953 plastic-envelope designs. Of the 1,308,400 pennies issued almost the total number were made up in sets in transparent plastic envelopes.

These sets were offered originally through the banks for 7*s*. 6*d*. per set. This, of course, excluded the crown piece.

The portrait of Elizabeth II as it appears on her pre-decimal coinage.

For several years these sets were not bought in any quantity, but in recent years they have been much sought after, and today are virtually unobtainable, except at greatly increased prices. At one time prices reached a peak figure of £15 per set in 1969. The forty thousand proof Coronation sets, however, were readily purchased in 1953 at 25*s*. each, but these, too, rose to a peak of £45 in the same year.

In 1954 all the previous denominations continued except the crown piece and the penny. One specimen penny with this date is known to exist in private hands, despite the

Royal Mint's declaration that there was no issue with this date. One cannot resist speculating what the value of this coin may be, now possessed by a United States company, the Paramount Coin Corporation, who at one time valued it at $30,000.

The alteration to the legend on the 1954 coins was the result of complying with the wishes of certain Commonwealth countries. This omission of 'BRITT.OMN' from the legend, which means, when translated with the word 'Regina', 'Queen of the British Empire', a phrase which was unacceptable to some countries of the Commonwealth.

It was found that retouching of both the 1953 and 1954 dies had taken place, creating only a slight but nevertheless noticeable difference between two types of several denominations.

By 1956 farthings were of little use, and it was decided that minting them should cease. The mintage figure for this year, being under 2 million, ultimately created a considerable demand from collectors. These now obsolete coins (they were demonetised in 1960) at the time of writing have a selling price of as much as 27s. 6d. for a brilliant uncirculated specimen.

It is reported that one of London's big banks cleared out all their farthings early in 1961 at face value; the consignment weighed over two tons! One cannot help wondering how the buyer has utilised them all (4,800 farthings weigh 30 lb. avoirdupois).

The over-production of pennies (perhaps more accurately described as the lack of public demand for them) in the

1940s caused the Mint to cease production temporarily after a very small issue in 1950, 1951, and the Coronation Year until 1961, when production was resumed. Half-pennies continued regularly each year until 1961, when none was produced. This was the first year that halfpennies had not been minted since 1849 and 1850. Today, of course, they are no longer legal tender, having been demonetised on 31st July 1969. The vast number of these not surrendered to the Royal Mint may be because some of them are being held back by would-be speculators.

In 1957 the Treasury sanctioned the issue of sovereigns with the bust of Elizabeth II. It is said that these were produced to counteract forged sovereigns that were being made on the Continent, believed to be of Italian origin. Other forged sovereigns were traced from Beirut. These forgeries, which were of good weight and of 22 carat gold, were being used for world trade. This situation was made possible by the genuine sovereign being more highly valued than its bullion content. As a result, British sovereigns, last used in 1918, were made legal tender again, thus making it a greater offence even for foreign forgers outside British law to forge gold coins that were current rather than obsolete.

In 1958 and 1959 more sovereigns were minted. These, together with the later 1957s, had a somewhat coarser milling than those of the earlier 1957s, making a total issue for these three years of over 13 million coins. This in effect counteracted the activities of forgers, most of whom operated through the bullion markets on the Continent. Production ceased in 1960 and 1961, but from 1962 to 1968 sovereigns have been minted regularly.

As a result of legislation to conserve the use of gold, the situation for the British collector has become rather ridiculous, and the law proves itself an Ass. On supposedly economic grounds a collector may not collect post-1837 gold coins unless he has a licence to do so. He is not permitted to hold this licence unless he possesses gold coins justifying his application. Alternatively, he must possess a

Heraldry overflows from the 1960 crown reverse, which is identical to the earlier Coronation crown.

substantial collection of other coins, then at the discretion of the Bank of England he may be granted a licence. For a member of the public the position is even worse. He may not hold a sovereign (nor any other gold coin) unless he possessed it before 26th April 1966. In that case he may hold up to four. Thus a beginner to coin collecting will be banned for ever from collecting gold coins unless the law is changed.

After an interval of seven years another crown, the 1960

issue, appeared. This coin had a similar obverse to the lower denominations and a reverse identical to the 1953 crown, except that the date was changed. This was specially struck for the British Exhibition in New York, where a large number of proof-like specimens, estimated at approximately 18,000, were sold; these are naturally in greater demand today than the ordinary strikings. The latter were circulated through the banks in the usual manner.

1965 Churchill crown.

On the death of Sir Winston Churchill another crown piece was issued in commemoration, 1965. The number manufactured exceeded any previous issue of crowns by a huge margin, 19,640,000 were issued. The obverse followed the normal Gillick design, whereas the reverse displayed the bust of Sir Winston with a typically determined expression. Oscar Nemon, the designer, portrays him in his famous war-time garment, the 'siren suit'.

After a lapse of seven years pennies were issued with the

1961 date, no halfpennies were minted—the first 'missing' year for 101 years. In the following year both these coins continued to be struck with a year date until 1967, this date being the last for the non-decimal coins.

In an attempt to stop investors hoarding the 1967 pre-decimal coins, the Chancellor of the Exchequer instructed the Royal Mint to 'freeze' the date as long as it was necessary. The result, except for the florins and shillings, which have been augmented by the 1968 five- and ten-pence, has been a vast overall mintage of the 1967 date.

Throughout the reign of Elizabeth II the Maundy coin sets continue to be in great demand, with a consequent rise in price. The 1953 Coronation set is widely sought after by collectors, a new 'type' being instituted in 1954, which forced the price up to the £100 mark. The major reason for interest in Elizabeth's Maundy money was caused by the restricted number of sets; they have scarcity value. The average yearly issue since 1953 is a little in excess of 1,100, which is a very minute figure compared to the number of possible collectors.

On 15th February 1968 the Royal Mint released details of the future decimal coinage, eight months after the decision had been made public.

The obverse of the new coinage bears the well-known figure of the Queen, a design by Arnold Machin that is also used for some of the Commonwealth countries. In an open competition artists were invited to submit designs for the reverses to the Royal Mint Advisory Committee, eleven strong in number, over which the Duke of Edinburgh presided. From eighty-two submitted designs, a short list of fifteen was selected. Unlike the 1953 Coronation designs, for which two artists designed the obverses and two the reverses, Arnold Machin's design was exclusively selected for the obverse. The reverses were all entrusted to Christopher Ironside. In his designs the artist, however, left no room for the conventional position of the date. This was

The 50p, a coin that has received nothing but contempt from the public.

transferred to the obverse, where it created a slightly un-balanced effect on the inscription, since too many letters were positioned on the left side of the Queen's effigy in relation to those on the right. Apart from perhaps a rather unnatural heraldic lion on the 10 new pence, the designs in general are pleasing. Nationalistic feelings are gratified by presenting a national design of each country making up the British Isles.

The 50p (issued in October 1969) shows the seated figure of Britannia in modern style of design. The 10p displays a crowned British lion, passant guardant; the badge of Scotland and a crowned thistle decorate the 5p, and the 2p displays the Prince of Wales' feathers with the ICH DIEN on a scroll beneath. The Northern Ireland 2p, however, will be having a different design to this, some months after the commencement of the new coinage; the 1p shows a new design of the portcullis with a crown above—a rearrangement of the current 3d. nickel–brass piece, while the smallest coin, the ½p reveals the Royal Crown as the central design.

While there was a broad acceptance of these coins at the time of announcement, voices were raised against the method of selecting them. It is accepted that there has to be a considerable thinning-out of designs; it has even been suggested that the final half-dozen designs could have been publicly displayed, taking a general consensus of opinion before the final selection was to be made.

So as to acquaint the public with the decimal coins, sets of all the denominations (except the 50p) were on sale at 5s. 6d. per set. In addition to this, 10p and 5p pieces were released on 23rd April 1968 for circulation alongside the existing 2s. and 1s. pieces, which are of identical size and weight.

On 14th October 1969 the cupro-nickel 50p was released, taking the place of the 10s. Bank of England note. This coin is unusual. Its shape is seven-sided—its technical description being 'an equilateral curve heptagon'. The decision to adopt an odd-shaped coin may well have been to avoid the use of a third metal, e.g. brass, which easily discolours; for this reason it would be unacceptable to the majority of the public. Its shape makes it distinguishable from the other coins, irrespective of metal and colour. However, those who remember the half-sovereign look at the 50p and shake their heads. Fair comment indeed.

Prince Charles

Although Prince Charles does not qualify for a chapter as a monarch, however, as Prince of Wales and a future king, he merits a separate space, reserved here to give some detail

Prince Charles' portrait from the official Investiture medal issued in 1969.

of his personal history. Naturally no coinage has been issued bearing his effigy; nevertheless, a number of commemorative medals have been struck to record the Investiture, on 1st July, one unforgettable occasion of 1969.

Prince Charles was born on 14th November 1948 at Buckingham Palace, and was duly afforded the honours befitting the heir-apparent to the British throne.

His early rearing was entrusted in part to two Scots

'Nannies'—the late Miss Helen Lightbody and Miss Mabel Anderson; the Queen herself took an active part in his upbringing, as she has done with all her children, devoting special time to them daily. Throughout his education the policy has been to avoid, where possible, the isolation which may result from position of birth. Unlike his predecessors Edward VIII and George VI, every attempt has been taken to make his schooling and University career as normal as possible.

Charles's first lessons began at five years under another Scot, a Miss Peebles, entrusted with the task of finding his natural ability for the various subjects. At eight he became a pupil at Hill House School in Kensington—an early preparatory day school. From there he went to Cheam Preparatory School on the Berkshire downs—the school his father had attended as a junior. The general accent here, as in his next school, Gordonstoun, was to allow him to behave entirely as other boys. Judging by the results, it was a wise decision.

Undoubtedly his education at Gordonstoun and Timbertop in Australia was a major influence on his general outlook and broadened his experience.

At Trinity College, Cambridge, and during his short stay at Aberystwyth University he earned a reputation as a hard worker, achieving a standard well above average in the subjects of his choice. The Prince's studies had to be broken off for his Investiture as Prince of Wales.

His interviews on television have greatly impressed the public, and by general consent he is accepted as a very likeable young man.

Prince Charles—Medallions

To commemorate his investiture as Prince of Wales on 1st July 1969 a number of medallions were struck. The official issue was by the Royal Mint on behalf of the Welsh Office. A second struck by the Government's official bullion brokers, Johnson, Matthey & Co. Ltd., was under the authorisation of the Royal Borough of Caernarvon. Another nine firms, at least, produced medallions revealing an excellent variety of high-quality portraits. These were all struck mainly in silver and bronze but also in platinum, gold, and palladium, giving the very large interested public and the numerous overseas visitors a wide choice of selection as souvenirs of this magnificently displayed historic event. Particularly praiseworthy were the efforts of the sculptors to 'catch' the natural expression of the Prince.

To single out any one of these or to place them in order of merit would be merely the interpretation of individual opinion. The use of inscriptions in Welsh is a highly commendable idea, which supports those who are encouraging the wider use of the Welsh tongue.

The reverses have fully covered the emblems and badges of Wales, which are all suitable for the occasion. These are the royal badge of the Prince of Wales, the crowned badge of the last all-Welsh prince Gwynedd (now adopted as part of the Prince's personal badge in Wales), the three-plumed fleur-de-lis (in use since the time of the Black Prince), the Red Dragon (the badge of the ancient Welsh princes), and the beautiful architecture of Caernarvon Castle (the scene of the first Investiture in 1301, and the most recent in 1969).

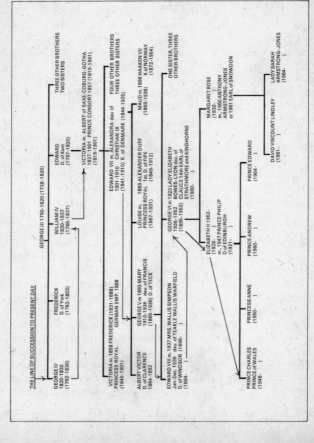

THE LINE OF SUCCESSION TO PRESENT DAY

GEORGE III 1760-1820 (1738-1820)

GEORGE IV
1820-1830
(1762-1830)

FREDERICK
D. of York
(1763-1803)

WILLIAM IV
1830-1837
(1765-1837)

EDWARD
D. of Kent
(1767-1820)

THREE OTHER BROTHERS
TWO SISTERS

VICTORIA m. ALBERT of SAXE-COBURG-GOTHA
1837-1901 PRINCE CONSORT 1857 (1819-1861)
(1819-1901)

VICTORIA m. 1858 FREDERICK (1831-1888)
PRINCESS ROYAL
(1840-1901)

GERMAN EMP. 1888

EDWARD VII m. ALEXANDRA dau of
1901-1910   CHRISTIAN IX
(1841-1910) K. of DENMARK
(1844-1925)

FOUR OTHER BROTHERS
THREE OTHER SISTERS

ALBERT VICTOR
D. of CLARENCE
1864-1892

GEORGE V m 1893 MARY
1910-1936 dau. of FRANCIS
(1865-1936) D. of TECK

LOUISE m. 1889 ALEXANDER DUFF
PRINCESS ROYAL 1st. D. of FIFE
(1867-1931)   (1849-1912)

MAUD. m. 1896 HAAKEN VII
(1869-1938) K. of NORWAY
(1872-1964)

ONE SISTER, THREE
OTHER BROTHERS

EDWARD VIII m. 1937 MRS. WALLIS SIMPSON
Jan-Dec. 1936 dau. of TEAKLE WALLIS WARFIELD
D. of WINDSOR (1896-
(1894-

GEORGE VI m 1923 LADY ELIZABETH
1936-1952 BOWES-LYON dau. of
(1895-1952) CLAUDE 14th EARL of
STRATHMORE and KINGHORNE
(1900-

MARGARET ROSE
(1930-
m. 1960 ANTHONY
ARMSTRONG-JONES
cr 1961 EARL of SNOWDON

ELIZABETH II 1952-
(1926-
m. 1947 PRINCE PHILIP
D. of EDINBURGH
(1921-

DAVID VISCOUNT LINDLEY
(1961-

LADY SARAH
ARMSTRONG-JONES
(1964-

PRINCE CHARLES
PRINCE of WALES
(1948-

PRINCESS ANNE
(1950-

PRINCE ANDREW
(1960-

PRINCE EDWARD
(1964-

A CONCISE CATALOGUE OF THE ENGLISH COINAGE FROM 1837 TO DATE, CONTAINING MINTAGE FIGURES, VARIETIES, AND COMPARATIVE NOTES

Quarter Farthings

Date	Mintage
VICTORIA (1837–1901)	

This tiny copper coin (12 mm.) was struck for use in Ceylon and was roughly equivalent to $\frac{1}{2}$ doit and $\frac{1}{2}$ Indian pie.

Date	Mintage
1839	3·6
1851	
1852	2·2
1853	

Third Farthings

Date	Mintage
VICTORIA (1837–1901)	

Copper

1844	
1844 RE	1·3

The RE variety had these letters instead of REG.

Bronze

1866	0·6
1868	0·1
1876	0·1
1878	0·3
1881	0·1
1884	0·1
1885	0·3

The very low mintage of these coins make prices relatively high. The various fractions of a farthing are referred to by collectors as 'FRACTIONALS'. Third farthings were for use in Malta, where three 'Maltese

Third Farthings—*continued*

Date	Mintage
EDWARD VII (1902–10)	
1902	0·3
GEORGE V (1911–36)	
1913	0·3

Grains' were equal to one English farthing. The two dates 1902 and 1913 are, in the writer's opinion, underestimated by collectors.

Half Farthings

Date	Mintage
VICTORIA (1837–1901)	
Copper	
1839	2·0
1842	—
1843	3·4
1844	
1844 E over N	6·5
1847	3·0
1851	—
1852	1·0
1853	1·0
1854	0·7
1856	0·9

The copper half-farthing is the commonest 'Fractional' and was made for use in CEYLON. Although they were made current in the United Kingdom in 1842, the half-farthing saw no great usage, and was demonetised in 1869. 1844 is a very common date.

Farthings

Date	Mintage
VICTORIA (1837–1901)	

Young Head Copper

Date	Mintage
1838	0·1
1839	4·3
1840	3·0
1841	1·7
1842	1·3
1843	4·1
1844	0·4
1845	3·2
1846	2·6
1847	3·9
1848	1·3
1849	0·6
1850	0·4?
1851 } 1851 'D'	1·9
1852	0·8
1853 W. W. R'sd } 1853 W. W. Inc.	1·0
1854	6·5
1855 W. W. R'sd } 1855 W. W. Inc.	3·4
1856	1·8
1857	1·1
1858	1·7
1859	1·3
1860	V. Rare

Unlike the above series, the 1844 farthing is rare, together with the 1851 'D' variety which has DRITANNIAR in place of BRITANNIAR. The young bust of Victoria was engraved by William Wyon—it is these initials that are referred to after the 1853 date.

Confusion is often caused by the copper 1860 farthing, which although not included in the official Mint report, does occasionally turn up.

(*Note:* Copper farthings have the date under Victoria's Head.)

Farthings—*continued*

Date	Mintage
Young Head Bronze	
1860 BD ⎫	
1860 TH ⎭	2·8
1861	8·6
1862	14·3
1863	1·4
1864	2·5
1865	4·6
1866	3·5
1867	5·0
1868	4·8
1869	3·2
1872	2·1
1873	3·2
1874H	3·6
1875	0·7
1875H	6·1
1876H	1·1
1878	4·0
1879	4·0
1880	1·8
1881	3·5
1881H	1·8
1882H	1·8
1883	1·1
1884	5·7
1885	5·4

The 1860/1 bronze varieties are extremely numerous, and only the major types with BEADED(BD) and TOOTHED(TH) borders are included here.

In the 1870s and 1880s the Mint was forced to 'contract out' some issues to a private mint (Heatons) in Birmingham. The small H Mint-mark appears on the farthing under the date on the reverse.

Although the silver and gold coinage changed in design in 1887, the bronze retained the Young or 'Bun Head'. The 1895 Young Head coin is quite rare while the Old—or Veiled— Head coins are common. The excellent Old Head (OH) bust was modelled by Thomas Brock and continued until the Queen's death in 1901.

Farthings—*continued*

Date	Mintage
1886	7·7
1887	1·3
1888	1·9
1890	2·1
1891	5·0
1892	0·9
1893	3·9
1894	2·4
1895 YH (inc. in OH)	

Old Head Bronze

1895 OH	2·8
1896	3·6
1897 Normal	4·6
1897 Black	
1898	4·0
1899	3·8
1900	6·0
1901	8·0

EDWARD VII (1902–10)

1902	5·1
1903	5·3
1904	3·6
1905	4·1
1906	5·3
1907	4·4

The Britannia reverse of a 1901 farthing.

From 1897 to 1917 the farthing was artificially toned, i.e. blackened to avoid confusion with the half-sovereign.

Farthings—*continued*

Date	Mintage
1908	4·3
1909	8·9
1910	2·6

GEORGE V (1911–36)

1911	5·2
1912	7·7
1913	4·2
1914	6·1
1915	7·1
1916	11·0
1917	21·4
1918	19·4
1919	15·1
1920	11·5
1921	9·5
1922	10·0
1923	8·0
1924	8·7
1925	12·6
1926	9·8
1927	7·9
1928	1·6
1929	8·4
1930	4·2
1931	6·6
1932	9·3

The years between 1916 and 1936 were filled with crisis, turmoil, and change. Farthings played a vital part in everyday economics, as the smallest coinage unit.

Hindenburg, MacDonald, Dollfuss, and Hitler became household names, and Edward VIII came and went in this period.

Farthings—*continued*

Date	Mintage
1933	4·6
1934	3·1
1935	2·2
1936	9·7

GEORGE VI (1937–52)

1937	8·1
1938	7·4
1939	31·4
1940	18·4
1941	27·3
1942	28·9
1943	22·2
1944	25·1
1945	23·7
1946	24·4
1947	14·7
1948	16·6
1949	8·4
1950	10·3
1951	14·0
1952	5·3

ELIZABETH II (1953–   )

1953	6·1
1954	6·6
1955	5·8
1956	2·0

The familiar Wren reverse from a 1949 farthing.

George VI was crowned in 1937, and gradually the 'Wren' farthing began to play less and less of a significant role.

After the Second World War when rationing ceased this small coin was little more than a nuisance.

The farthing was discontinued in the fourth year of Elizabeth's reign and was demonetised in 1961. The 1956 coin is scarce.

Halfpennies

Date	Mintage
VICTORIA (1837–1901)	

Young Head Copper

Date	Mintage
1838	0·4
1839	Proofs only
1841	1·1
1843	1·0
1844	1·1
1845	1·1
1846	0·8
1847	0·7
1848 } 1848/7 }	3·2
1851 } 1851 DOTS }	0·2
1852 } 1852 DOTS }	0·6
1853 } 1853/2 }	1·5
1854	12·3
1855	1·4
1856	2·0
1857 } 1857 DOTS }	1·2
1858 } 1858/6 } 1858/7 } 1858 Sm date }	2·4

Victoria's copper halfpennies bore the Wyon portrait on the obverse and a modified version of the reverse, as used by George IV (1820–30) and William IV (1830–37). The legend changed from REX (L. King) to REG (L. Regina—Queen). Publications often show a Victorian halfpenny (or penny and farthing) with the wrong reverse of the previous reigns—it is a point worth looking for.

Date	Mintage
1859 ⎫	
1859/8 ⎭	1·3
1860	V. rare

Young Head Bronze

1860 BD ⎫	
1860 TH ⎭	6·6
1861 Sig. ⎫	
1861 No Sig. ⎭	54·1
1862	61·1
1863	16·0
1864	0·5
1865 ⎫	
1865/3 ⎭	0·8
1866	2·5
1867	2·5
1868	3·0
1869	3·2
1870	4·3
1871	1·0?
1872	4·7
1873	3·4
1874	1·3
1874 H	5·0
1875	5·4
1875 H	1·2

See note on farthings discussing 1860 issues.

Darwin, Garibaldi, Lincoln, and Bismarck figured prominently in the news of this period, while nearer home bronze replaced copper in the small change. The Bun Head halfpennies are a static uninspiring series and are difficult to acquire in top condition. In fact, now that the halfpenny has been demonetised they will be difficult to get in *any* condition. The 1871 and the 1865 over 3 coins are the 'key' dates to this series.

Date	Mintage
1876 H	5·8
1878	1·4
1879	3·6
1880	2·4
1881	2·0
1881 H	1·7
1882 H	4·5
1883	3·0
1884	7·0
1885	8·6
1886	8·6
1887	10·7
1888	6·8
1889 1889/8	7·7
1890	11·2
1891	13·2
1892	2·5
1893	7·2
1894	1·7

Old Head Bronze

Date	Mintage
1895	3·0
1896	9·1
1897	8·7
1898	8·6

1894 saw the opening of the Manchester Ship Canal and also provides us with a very scarce halfpenny. Another coin to have a close look at is the 1899, with the possibility it might be of the overdate type, i.e. with the 9 struck over the 8 of the previous year.

The Old Head halfpennies are quite common.

Date	Mintage
1899	12·1
1900	13·8
1901	11·1

EDWARD VII (1902–10)

1902	
1902 (low tide) }	13·7
1903	11·4
1904	8·1
1905	10·1
1906	11·1
1907	16·8
1908	16·6
1909	8·3
1910	10·8

GEORGE V (1911–36)

1911	12·6
1912	21·2
1913	·17·5
1914	20·3
1915	21·6
1916	39·4
1917	38·2
1918	22·3
1919	28·1
1920	35·1

Edward VII came on to the throne in 1902 in the same year that the Boer War ended. The low-tide variety was caused by the use of a few dies of previous years when the horizon reached half-way up Britannia's leg. New dies were subsequently engraved with a 'high-tide'.

Halfpennies from 1911 to 1936 are very scarce in brilliant uncirculated condition. This fact is perhaps due to the fact that it had the significance and usage of the penny by today's standards, and were spent rather than saved. Now that they have been withdrawn, the rare or key-date coins will gradually increase in significance.

Date	Mintage
1921	28·0
1922	10·7
1923	12·3
1924	14·0
1925 (1924 type) } 1925 (1926 type) }	12·2
1926	6·7
1927	15·6
1928	20·9
1929	25·7
1930	12·5
1931	16·1
1932	14·4
1933	10·6
1934	7·7
1935	12·2
1936	23·0

GEORGE VI (1937–52)

Date	Mintage
1937	24·5
1938	40·3
1939	28·9
1940	32·2
1941	45·1
1942	71·9
1943	76·2
1944	81·8

One of the commonest halfpennies of George VI kept by collectors is the 1937 date, which frequently turns up in mint condition—probably kept as a souvenir after the Coronation. The 1946 is classed as a scarce date, even with an official mintage figure of 22,725,600.

Reverse of a 1952 halfpenny. The year in which George VI died. The ship is the *Golden Hind*.

Halfpennies—*continued*

Date	Mintage
1945	57·0
1946	22·7
1947	21·3
1948	26·9
1949	24·7
1950	24·2
1951	14·9
1952	33·3

ELIZABETH II (1953–   )

1953	8·9
1954	19·4
1955	18·5
1956	21·8
1957	39·7
1958	66·3
1959	79·2
1960	41·3
1962	41·8
1963	42·7
1964	78·6
1965	98·1
1966	95·3
1967	100·3

The two decades between 1947 and 1967 saw vast changes in world technology and the gradual extinction of the bronze halfpenny. As half an old penny went out, half a new penny came in, and a vicious circle has been completed.

Pennies

Date	Mintage

VICTORIA (1837–1901)

Young Head Copper

Date	Mintage
1839	Proofs exist
1841 Reg: ⎫ 1841 No: ⎭	0·9
1843 Reg: ⎫ 1843 No: ⎭	0·5
1844	0·2
1845	0·3
1846 Far: ⎫ 1846 Near: ⎭	0·5
1847 Far: ⎫ 1847 Near: ⎭	0·4
1848 ⎫ 1848/6 ⎬ 1848/7 ⎭	0·1
1849	0·2
1851 Far: ⎫ 1851 Near: ⎭	0·5
1853 Far: ⎫ 1853 Near: ⎭	1·0
1854/3 ⎫ 1854 Far: ⎬ 1854 Near: ⎭	6·7
1855 Far: ⎫ 1855 Near: ⎭	5·2

Victoria married Prince Albert in 1840, and it was not until the following year that any copper pennies were made for circulation. Many varieties exist with over-dates and 'far-' and 'near-' colons in the legend.

1854 saw the start of the Crimean War. There was also the largest mintage issuing, therefore the commonest of the pennies. It is also likely that part of the issue in 1855 may have been made up of coins given the previous year date. The spectacular 1860 over 59 penny is rare in any condition, and is much prized by collectors.

Date	Mintage
1856 Far:	
1856 Near:	1·2
1857 Far:	
1857 Near:	0·7
1857 Sm. Date	
1858	
1858/3	
1858/6	1·6
1858/7	
1858 Sm. Date	
1858 No WW	
1859	1·0
1859 Sm. Date	
1860	—

Young Head Bronze

1860 BD	
1860 TH	5·0
1861 Sig.	
1861 No Sig.	36·5
1862	50·5
1863	28·1
1864 Plain 4	
1864 Cr'slt 4	3·4
1865	
1865/3	8·6
1866	10·0

Young Head Copper

This riband is not part of the final design, but has been caused by clashed dies. It is found on copper ¼d, ½d, and 1d of early type.

Young Head Copper—riband variety.

Prince Albert died in 1861, and Victoria's outlook on life was drastically changed. By 1861, the change from copper to bronze was in full swing, with a new Wyon portrait on the obverse.

Date	Mintage
1867	5·5
1868	1·2
1869	2·6?
1870	5·7
1871	1·3
1872	8·5
1873	8·5
1874 '73 Type 1874 New Head	5·6
1874 H '73 Type 1874 H New Head	6·7
1875	10·7
1875 H	0·7
1876 H	11·1
1877	9·6
1878	2·8
1879	7·7
1880	3·0
1881 1881 New	2·3
1881 H	3·8
1882 H	7·5
1883	6·2
1884	11·7
1885	7·1
1886	6·1
1887	5·3

The 'bun' pennies are very popular with collectors, who endeavour to obtain one coin of each date. The Suez Canal was formally opened in 1869, and although there was supposed to be a mintage of 2,580,480, this date is very rare. The 1865 over 3 has long been under-rated, but a mint specimen was offered in 1969 at £1,000 by a London company. The designs of both obverse and reverse were modified spasmodically, but did not alter in type until 1894/5.

Pennies—*continued*

Date	Mintage
1888	5·1
1889	12·6
1890	15·3
1891	17·9
1892	10·5
1893	8·2
1894	3·9

Old Head Bronze

1895 2 MM ⎫	
1895 ⎭	5·4
1896	24·1
1897	20·7
1898	14·3
1899	26·4
1900	31·8
1901	22·2

EDWARD VII (1902–10)

1902 ⎫	
1902 (low tide) ⎭	27·0
1903	21·4
1904	12·9
1905	17·8
1906	38·0
1907	47·3
1908	31·5
1909	19·6
1910	29·5

The two-millimetre (2MM) variety is not very easy to spot, but under a magnifying glass you should be able to see the different distances between Britannia's trident and the letter P of PENNY in the legend. For an explanation of the high and low tides see the halfpenny tables.

Pennies—*continued*

Date	Mintage
GEORGE V (1911–36)	
1911	23·1
1912	48·3
1912 H	16·8
1913	65·5
1914	50·8
1915	47·3
1916	86·4
1917	107·9
1918	84·2
1918 H 1918 KN	3·7
1919	113·8
1919 H 1919 KN	5·2
1920	124·7
1921	129·7
1922	16·3
1926 1926 ME	4·5
1927	61·0
1928	50·2
1929	49·1
1930	29·1
1931	19·8
1932	8·3
1933*	

An enlargement of the exergue of a 1918 Kings Norton penny. (The exergue is the portion of the coin beneath the line, under which the date appears). Note the odd shape of the 'K'.

Whenever the Royal Mint were unable to meet the demand, some of their work was carried out by private provincial concerns, two of which were the Heaton and Kings Norton Mints in Birmingham (H and KN mint marks).

*A specimen sold in London, March 19th, 1969, for £3,600.

Date	Mintage
1934	14·0
1935	56·1
1936	154·3

GEORGE VI (1937–52)

1937	88·9
1938	121·6
1939	55·6
1940	42·3
1944	42·6
1945	79·5
1946	66·9
1947	52·2
1948	64·0
1949	14·3
1950	0·2
1951	0·1

ELIZABETH II (1953–)

1953	1·3
1961	48·3
1962	157·6
1963	119·7
1964	153·3
1965	121·3
1966	165·8
1967	155·3

The group of pennies from 1919 to 1963 listed here contain several pieces of great interest to collectors—the rare 1933 date; the new or modified 1926 penny; the artificially darkened pennies of the mid-forties; the rare 1950, 1951, and 1953 dates, and the unique 1954 date. This latter trial piece, although unlisted here, does exist and belongs to an American Corporation. An offer of £9,000 from a British company is reputed to have been turned down. No pennies were made for circulation between 1954 and 1960.

The 1967 date was frozen for pennies issued in 1968/9, and is thus one of our commonest coins in circulation.

Silver Three-halfpence ($1\frac{1}{2}d.$)

Date	Mintage
VICTORIA (1837–1901)	

1838	
1839	
1840	
1841	Mint report vague
1842	
1843	
1860	
1862	

This odd little coin—the $1\frac{1}{2}d.$ piece, was issued for use in Ceylon, British Guiana, and the British West Indies, all of which used our currency. These coins would not have been used here in Britain.

Threepences—Silver

Date	Mintage
VICTORIA (1837–1901)	

Young Head

1838	1·2
1839	0·6
1840	0·6
1841	0·4
1842	—
1843	2·0
1844	1·0
1845	1·3
1846	0·05
1849	0·1
1850	1·0

Silver threepences were among the first coins issued in Victoria's reign, and both currency and Royal Maundy coins had similar designs. It is for this reason that the threepence is occasionally missing from Maundy sets—the recipients spent them.

Date	Mintage
1851	0·5
1853	0·03
1854	1·5
1855	0·4
1856	1·0
1857	1·8
1858	1·4
1859	3·6
1860	3·4
1861	3·3
1862	1·2
1863	1·0
1864	1·3
1865	1·7
1866	1·9
1867	0·7
1868	
1868 R.R. }	1·5
1870	1·3
1871	1·0
1872	1·3
1873	4·1
1874	4·4
1875	3·3
1876	1·8
1877	2·6
1878	2·4

The silver threepence is one of the most consistent of Victorian issues, but regrettably one of the least sought after. Varieties are few and far between, but the 1868 RRITANNIAR error speaks for itself and is naturally quite rare. The 1887 Young Head coinage was always scarce, while the reverse is true of the Jubilee issue for that year. This generalisation is wrong in the case of the silver threepence, which is quite difficult to acquire in any condition.

Threepences—Silver—_continued_

Date	Mintage
1879	3·1
1880	1·6
1881	3·2
1882	0·5
1883	4·4
1884	3·3
1885	5·2
1886	6·2
1887	2·8

The real rarity of the silver threepenny pieces is the 1893 Jubilee date, a coin worth in excess of £100 in mint condition.

Jubilee Head

1887	Inc. in YH
1888	0·5
1889	4·6
1890	4·5
1891	6·3
1992	2·6
1893	3·1

Old Head

1893	Inc. in JH
1894	1·6
1895	4·8
1896	4·6
1897	4·5
1898	4·6

Date	Mintage
1899	6·2
1900	10·6
1901	6·1

EDWARD VII (1902–10)

1902	8·3
1903	5·2
1904	3·6
1905	3·5
1906	3·2
1907	4·8
1908	8·2
1909	4·1
1910	4·6

At one time it was a simple matter of placing a classified newspaper advertisement and you could obtain 5,000 silver 3d.'s for 6d. each. Today the situation is very different, with dealers selling individual coins by date, at very high prices. The coins of Edward VII are exceedingly difficult to obtain in Extremely Fine and Uncirculated grades.

GEORGE V (1911–36)

1911	5·8
1912	8·9
1913	7·1
1914	6·7
1915	5·5
1916	18·6
1917	21·7
1918	20·6
1919	16·8
1920	16·7
1921	8·7

Date	Mintage
1922	8·0
1925	3·7
1926	
1926 M.E.	4·1
1927 Proof 15022	
1928	1·3
1930	1·3
1931	6·3
1932	5·9
1933	5·6
1934	7·4
1935	7·0
1936	3·2

GEORGE VI (1937–52)

1937	8·1
1938	6·4
1939	1·4
1940	7·9
1941	8·0
1942	4·1
1943	1·4
1944	2·0
1945 Whole issue melted	

The M.E. or Modified Effigy type bears as the name implies the later bust of George V. The reverse (tail) of the threepence was altered from a plain figure '3' in a wreath to three oak sprigs in 1927, when only proof coins were issued in the sets. In 1937 the reverse was redesigned yet again, featuring a shield of St. George on a Tudor Rose. Brass threepenny 'bits' were issued from this year on, and by 1944 the silver coin was obsolete and discontinued. A rare 1937 brass pattern coin exists bearing the portrait of Edward VIII, who abdicated that year.

Threepences—Brass

Date	Mintage
GEORGE VI (1937–52)	
1937	45·7
1938	14·5
1939	5·6
1940	12·6
1941	60·2
1942	103·2
1943	101·7
1944	69·8
1945	33·9
1946	0·6
1948	4·2
1949	0·5
1950	1·6
1951	1·2
1952	25·5
ELIZABETH II (1953–)	
1953	30·6
1954	41·7
1955	41·1
1956	36·8
1957	24·3
1958	20·5
1959	28·5
1960	83·1
1961	41·1

The familiar threepenny bit has no decimal equivalent, and because of its shape and bulk will easily be withdrawn from circulation. Key-date coins are those of 1938, 1939, 1946, 1949, 1950, and 1951, all of which are scarce, even in 'Fine' condition.

The thrift plant reverse of the 1949 brass threepence. The date which is becoming very rare due to its low mintage.

Date	Mintage
1962	51·5
1963	35·3
1964	47·4
1965	24·0
1966	53·8
1967	100·3

Certain dates of the Elizabeth series are very difficult to find in brilliant uncirculated, e.g. 1958.

Groats (Silver 4*d.*)

Date	Mintage
VICTORIA (1837–1901)	
1838	2·2
1839	1·5
1840	1·5
1841	0·3
1842	0·7
1843	1·8
1844	0·9
1845	0·9
1846	1·4
1847/6	0·2
1848 ⎫ 1848/6 ⎬	0·7
1849	0·4
1851	0·6
1852	0·03

The groat is often confused with the Maundy 4*d.* The former bears the seated figure of Britannia and the latter a figure '4' within a laurel wreath.

The coin was originally designed for use in British Guiana to replace the ¼ guilder. From the large number found in this country, it is evident it had a wide circulation here. One Jubilee head coin was issued, dated 1888.

Groats (Silver 4d.)—*continued*

Date	Mintage
1853	0·01
1854	1·1
1855	0·6
1856	(95,000)
1888	(JH)

Sixpences

Date	Mintage
VICTORIA (1837–1901)	

Young Head

Date	Mintage
1838	1·6
1839	3·3
1840	2·1
1841	1·4
1842	0·6
1843	3·2
1844	4·0
1845	3·7
1846	4·3
1848	0·6
1850	0·5
1851	2·3
1853	3·8
1854	0·8
1855	1·1

In my opinion, the sixpences of the Victorian era are not of any great interest, but it must not be overlooked that in style and type they are a very consistent series. Sixpences were issued practically every year of Victoria's reign, with three distinct types—Young head, Jubilee head and Old head types. The earlier coins show much superior relief, while coins dated between 1864 and 1879 bear a small number over the date (called

Date	Mintage
1856	2·8
1857	2·2
1858	1·9
1859	4·7
1860	1·1
1862	1·0
1863	0·5
1864	4·3
1865	1·6
1866 Die No 1866 No Die No }	5·1
1867	1·4
1868	1·1
1869	0·4
1870	0·5
1871 Die No 1871 No Die No }	3·7
1872	3·4
1873	4·6
1874	4·2
1875	3·3
1876	0·8
1877	4·1
1878 1878 DR }	2·6
1879 Die No 1879 No Die No }	3·3

the die number) to determine the life of any given die.

The major variety of the group of sixpences listed here is the 1878 'DR' type, where the legend reads: VICTORIA DEI GRATIA DRITTANNIAR : REG : F : D : instead of 'BRITTANNIAR'. This error was probably due to the impromptu task on the part of the Royal Mint of providing coinage for Cyprus, ceded to Britain in that year. This is supported by the fact that the error only went through the first three dies, or rather, the highest die number recorded so far, with the error, is numbered '3'. 1882 is the scarcest of the latter issues, followed closely by the 1887 Young Head coin.

Date	Mintage
1880	3·9
1881	6·2
1882	0·8
1883	5·0
1884	3·4
1885	4·6
1886	2·7
1887	3·7

Jubilee Head

Date	Mintage
1887 WD	Inc. in YH
1887 WR	
1888	4·2
1889	8·7
1890	9·4
1891	7·0
1892	6·2
1893	Inc. in OH

Old Head

Date	Mintage
1893	7·4
1894	3·5
1895	7·0
1896	6·7
1897	5·0
1898	6·0

On June 21st, 1887, Victoria celebrated her Golden Jubilee, having reigned for fifty years. Many medals were issued as a tribute to the ageing Queen. In addition, the gold and silver coinages were redesigned, using a portrait by Joseph Boehm. There are two distinct types of 1887 'Jubilee' sixpences, shown here as 'WD' and 'WR', one the withdrawn, and its replacement, the 'wreath' type. The reverse of the first issue bore a very close resemblance to the shield reverse of the half-sovereign, and it was not long before the former were gilded and foisted on the public. Immediately the Mint became aware of this a new design with the words 'six pence' in

Date	Mintage
1899	8·0
1900	9·0
1901	5·1

EDWARD VII (1902–10)

1902	6·4
1903	5·4
1904	4·5
1905	4·2
1906	7·6
1907	8·7
1908	6·7
1909	6·6
1910	12·5

GEORGE V (1911–36)

1911	9·2
1912	11·0
1913	7·6
1914	22·7
1915	15·7
1916	22·2
1917	7·7
1918	27·6
1919	13·4
1920	14·1
1921	30·3

a wreath was substituted and the early type was withdrawn. In contrast to the common 1887 date, the last sixpence in the jubilee era, the 1893, is very rare, especially in top condition.

Ironically, the thirty-odd years covered by the sixpenny listing here changed the whole pattern of the world, and yet the humble 'tanner' remained as static and unaffected as ever. Of the four changes that did occur, the alteration in the fineness of the silver coinage was perhaps the most significant. In the early years copper was evident in the coins even when they had suffered a minimal amount of wear. With this and other problems in mind, the coinage was altered in design in

Date	Mintage
1922	16·9
1923	6·4
1924	17·4
1925	12·7
1926 1926 ME }	21·8
1927	68·9
1928	23·1
1929	28·3
1930	17·0
1931	16·9
1932	9·4
1933	22·2
1934	9·3
1935	14·0
1936	24·4

GEORGE VI (1937–52)

1937	22·3
1938	13·4
1939	28·7
1940	20·9
1941	23·1
1942	44·9
1943	46·9
1944	38·0
1945	40·0

1926/7. The oak-sprig reverse used between 1927 and 1936 carries the unusual abbreviation A.D. for Anno Domini (1927), a feature never normally found on British coins. The first sixpence of George VI bore the monogram G.R.I. which stood for George Rex Imperator, i.e. Emperor of India, a title dropped after 1948, when Independence was granted.

In 1947 the shortage of silver, combined with other economic factors, forced the Government to take drastic steps in altering the composition of all the silver coinage for circulation. In fact, the new coins had no silver in them at all, and were composed of 75% copper and 25% nickel. Our

Date	Mintage
1946	43·5
1947	30·0
1948	88·3
1948	41·4
1950	32·7
1951	40·4
1952	1·0

ELIZABETH II (1953–   )

1953	70·3
1954	105·2
1955	110·0
1956	110·0
1957	105·6
1958	123·5
1959	93·1
1960	103·3
1961	115·0
1962	178·3
1963	113·0
1964	152·2
1965	127·8
1966	175·7
1967	72·5

coinage was at least 'token', i.e. the intrinsic value of the coins themselves bore no relation to their face value. The 1952 sixpence is officially classified as a key-date coin sought after by collectors because of its low mintage. Although there is no single equivalent to the sixpence in decimal coinage ($2\frac{1}{2}$p), the enormous mintages of the Queen Elizabeth II issues shows how popular a coin it really is.

Shillings (1s.)

Date	Mintage
VICTORIA (1837–1901)	

Young Head

Date	Mintage
1838	2·0
1839	5·7
1840	1·6
1841	0·9
1842	2·1
1843	1·5
1844	4·5
1845	4·1
1846	4·0
1848/6	1·0
1849	0·6
1850	0·7
1851	0·5
1852	1·3
1853	4·3
1854	0·6
1855	1·4
1856	3·2
1857	2·6
1858	3·1
1859	4·6
1860	1·7
1861	1·4
1862	1·0
1863	0·9

There are some very rare Young Head shillings, especially in the early series up to the mid-1850s. It is surprising to both collector and dealer how few of these shillings really exist in better than V.F. condition.

In numerous cases throughout minting history there has been a need to economise in both production and metals utilised. It was just such an economy that produced the first coin listed here, the '1848 over 6', a coin that is not strictly a variety, as it is the only kind known of that date. 'Overdate' coins were, as the name implies, coins made from dies of previous years with the new date recut over it. This was a common practice in Victorian times and many overdates are recorded, especially in the copper penny series pre-1860. Dates like 1850, 51,

Date	Mintage
1864	4·5
1865	5·6
1866	5·0
1867	2·2
1868	3·3
1869	0·7
1870	1·5
1871	4·9
1872	8·9
1873	6·5
1874	5·5
1875	4·4
1876	1·1
1877	3·0
1878	3·1
1879	3·6
1880	4·8
1881	5·3
1882	1·6
1883	7·3
1884	4·0
1885	3·3
1886	2·1
1887	4·0

54 are always underpriced in catalogues, and are seldom found in any condition. The numbering of dies was carried out between 1864 and 1879, and proof coins are known of several dates, e.g. 1853, 1871, and 1880. Coins dated 1882 are scarce, and in fact, on the rarity scale used by collectors, it is classed as 'R^2' (see glossary for explanation).

The Jubilee-head design by Boehm was never very popular with the public, mainly because the tiny crown worn by the queen looked so ridiculous. Oman sums up the whole design in *The Coinage of England* as follows: '. . . an ill-balanced composition, with too much draped bust bedecked with orders and jewellery, a

Date	Mintage
Jubilee Head	
1887	Inc. Y.H.
1888	4·5
1889 S.H. ⎫	7·0
1889 L.H. ⎭	
1890	8·8
1891	5·7
1892	4·6
Old Head	
1894	6·0
1895	8·9
1896	9·3
1897	6·3
1898	9·8
1899	11·0
1900	11·0
1901	3·4
EDWARD VII (1902–10)	
1902	7·8
1903	2·0
1904	2·0
1905	0·4
1906	10·7
1907	14·0

skimpy veil covering a small part of the back of the head, and a ridiculously small imperial arched crown perched perilously on the royal head.' By popular demand, the jubilee designs were dropped in 1893/4 and a new, far superior bust, modelled by Thomas Brock, was accepted and used. At this point in time the copper coinage was brought into line with that of the silver and gold, and was given the old head in place of the long-running young or bun head.

When Edward VII was crowned in 1902 a proof set was issued with a matt-finish; therefore, strictly speaking, two types of 1902 shilling exist. Of all this short series the 1905 is the scarcest, followed by the 1903 and 1904 dates, all of which are in great demand.

There is a large group of

Shillings (1s.)—*continued*

Date	Mintage
1908	3·8
1909	5·6
1910	26·5

GEORGE V (1911–36)

Date	Mintage
1911	20·0
1912	15·5
1913	9·0
1914	23·4
1915	39·2
1916	35·8
1917	22·2
1918	35·9
1919	10·8
1920	22·8
1921	22·6
1922	27·2
1923	14·5
1924	9·2
1925	5·4
1926 1926 Me }	22·5
1927 Old 1927 New }	9·2
1928	18·1
1929	19·3
1930	3·1

dedicated collectors who collect the shilling series, from 1911 to date; I should say 'up to 1966', for no shillings were made with the 1967 date, as they were superseded by the 5p. Vast numbers of the 'pre-twenty' shillings have been taken out of circulation by collectors and dealers over the last few years, and many are still available in about 'Fine' condition. This is more than can be said for coins dated between 1921 and 1926, which deteriorated quickly once the copper alloy began to rear its ugly yellowish head. Due to this detrimental wear, far less of this latter group have weathered the ravages of time and are consequently in short supply in top condition.

In 1937 we see a fantastic change in the whole aspect of the humble 'bob', with the introduction of two entirely separate designs for English

Shillings (1s.)—*continued*

Date	Mintage
1931	6·9
1932	12·1
1933	11·5
1934	6·1
1935	9·1
1936	11·9

E

GEORGE VI (1937–52)

Date		Mintage
1937	E	8·3
	S	6·7
1938	E	4·8
	S	4·7
1939	E	11·0
	S	10·2
1940	E	11·0
	S	9·9
1941	E	11·4
	S	8·1
1942	E	17·5
	S	13·7
1943	E	11·4
	S	9·8
1944	E	11·6
	S	11·0
1945	E	15·1
	S	15·1

S

1937 shilling reverses. E—English and S—Scottish, the latter being a new innovation.

Date	Mintage
1946 E	18·7
S	16·4
1947 E	12·1
S	12·2
1948 E	45·6
S	45·4
1949 E	19·3
S	21·2
1950 E	19·2
S	14·3
1951 E	10·0
S	11·0

Elizabeth II (1953–

1953 E	41·9
S	20·7
1954 E	30·3
S	26·8
1955 E	45·3
S	28·0
1956 E	44·9
S	42·9
1957 E	42·8
S	18·0
1958 E	14·4
S	40·8

(E) and Scottish (S) coins respectively. The division was instituted as a compliment to the Queen.

The portrait on all of the English coins of George VI was designed by T. H. Paget. Engravers' initials have appeared on coins regularly since the times of Ancient Greece, when coins were more properly considered to be works of art. Artists have always had an immense influence on numismatics, with names like Cellini, Roettier, Pistrucci, and Wyon, asserting a great influence on the coinage of their day. With modern coining methods new disciplines have had to be learnt, and names like McKennal, Gray, Gardner, Paget and Gillick can all be found by careful scrutiny of those inconspicuous but significant initials, tucked away in the designs of most of our coins.

Date		Mintage
1959	E	19·4
	S	1·0
1960	E	27·0
	S	14·4
1961	E	39·8
	S	2·8
1962	E	36·7
	S	19·0
1963	E	44·7
	S	32·3
1964	E	8·6
	S	5·2
1965	E	9·2
	S	2·8
1966	E	15·0
	S	15·6
1967		None issued

A 1959 Scottish shilling, which is considered a scarce date, having a low mintage.

Florins (2s.)

Date	Mintage
VICTORIA (1837–1901)	
Young Head (*Gothic*)	
1849	0·4
1851	(1,540)
1852	1·0
1853	3·9
1854	0·6
1855	0·8
1856	2·2
1857	1·7
1858	2·2
1859	2·6
1860	1·5
1862	0·6
1863	0·9
1864	1·9
1865	1·6
1866	0·9
1867	0·4
1868	0·9
1870	1·1
1871	3·4
1872	7·2
1873	5·9
1874	1·6
1875	1·1
1876	0·6

The 'Gothic' florin was our first practical step towards a decimal currency, actually lauding the fact in its reverse legend as 'ONE FLORIN ONE TENTH OF A POUND'. The 1848 coins were never issued for circulation and are classed as patterns. The 1849 coin is as common as its predecessor is rare. The omission of the Christian 'DEI GRATIA' (by the grace of God) from the legend is reputed to have offended many an orthodox parishioner throughout the country. Consequently the 'Godless' coins, as they were called, were amended in design and from 1851 until 1887 the date was written in roman numerals. There were many pattern or trial pieces mainly by Wyon in the early years, and such names as ONE CENTUM, ONE DECADE, ONE DIME, and ONE CENTUM were used to signify decimal parentage. It is interesting to

Date	Mintage
1877	
1877 (No WW)	} 0·7
1878	1·8
1879	
1879 (No WW)	} 1·5
1880	3·6
1881	
1881 (xxri)	} 2·6
1883	3·6
1884	1·5
1885	1·8
1886	0·6
1887	1·8

Jubilee Head

1887 Inc. in YH	
1888	1·5
1889	3·0
1890	1·7
1891	0·8
1892	0·3

Old Head

1893	1·7
1894	2·0
1895	2·2
1896	3·0

note that the florin and shilling were the first coins directly translated into the decimal system and issued for circulation. The change from two shillings to ten new pence is a mere face-lift, evolved one hundred and twenty years ago. Such is life.

The redesigned florin seems to have lost the charm of its predecessor and the alteration of the lettering to the Gothic style detracts from, instead of enchanting, the overall theme of the piece. For generations these post-1851 coins have confused the public, mainly because they are so unorthodox in their appearance. Most dates are exceptionally rare in uncirculated condition, and certain dates like 1851, 1853, 1863 are hardly ever offered for public sale. The Jubilee design was imposed upon the florin in 1887, together with a completely new reverse. The new coin had cruciform shields separated by sceptres in the

Florins (2s.)—*continued*

Date	Mintage
1897	1·7
1898	3·0
1899	4·0
1900	5·5
1901	2·6

EDWARD VII (1902–10)

1902	2·1
1903	1·9
1904	2·7
1905	1·1
1906	6·9
1907	5·9
1908	3·2
1909	3·4
1910	5·6

GEORGE V (1911–36)

1911	5·9
1912	8·5
1913	4·5
1914	21·1
1915	12·3
1916	21·0
1917	11·1
1918	29·2
1919	9·4

angles, with a star of the garter in the centre—a layout once described as consisting of tea-trays and pokers! Both 1891 and 1892 dates are very scarce—especially in perfect condition.

The Old or Veiled Head florins were introduced when it was decided that the Jubilee designs had outlived their usefulness. The obverse was excellent, portraying the queen precisely as she was visualised by the masses, while the reverse was a disjointed mess of shields, sceptres, symbols and legend seemingly thrown together.

Although Edward VII's reign was comparatively short, the whole coinage (with the exception, perhaps, of the 1902 ½ farthing, which should not really count) has a fluency of style that was found lacking in his mother's whole coinage. The *piéce de resistance* of the Edward series is the florin, with a defiant Britannia, standing on

Florins (2s.)—*continued*

Date	Mintage
1920	15·3
1921	34·8
1922	23·8
1923	21·5
1924	4·5
1925	1·4
1926	5·1
1927	0·1
1928	11·0
1929	16·3
1930	5·7
1931	6·5
1932	0·7
1933	8·6
1835	7·5
1936	9·8

GEORGE VI (1937–52)

Date	Mintage
1937	13·0
1938	7·9
1939	20·8
1940	18·7
1941	24·4
1942	39·8
1943	26·7
1944	27·5
1945	25·8

the prow of a ship, probably a trireme, with the sea in the background. It is worthwhile pausing for a moment to consider the possible propaganda value of this treatment, for it was the first time ever that this elegant figure had risen from her seated position on the coin of the realm. With the world in a turmoil, the balance of power changing and the Empire slipping slowly from our grasp, it may have been one way of saying that 'Britain ruled the waves'. There is also the possibility that this design was used to convey Edward's own strong links with the sea.

From 1911 to 1925 the reverse of the florin was back to tea-tray shields and poker-like sceptres; the only change of note in the coins was that of the alloy, in 1920. The dates of 1911, 1912, and 1913 are quite scarce today in the better grades, while coins of 1925, 1927, and 1932 are rare in any condition.

Florins (2s.)—*continued*

Year	Value
1946	22·3
1947	22·9
1948	67·5
1949	28·6
1950	24·3
1951	27·4

ELIZABETH II (1953–   )

Year	Value
1953	11·9
1954	13·0
1955	25·8
1956	47·8
1957	33·0
1958	9·5
1959	14·0
1960	13·8
1961	37·5
1962	35·1
1963	25·6
1964	16·5
1965	48·2
1966	84·0
1967	72·5

Bertram McKennal's bust was used throughout the reign, and was modified in 1926/7 giving a fuller and improved portrait. The reverse used from 1927 to 1936 was only marginally better than its predecessor, while the reverse used for George VI's coins was, if anything, worse. Kruger Gray unsuccessfully attempted to simplify the coin, and in doing so, produced a more cumbersome design than before. Then in 1953 a far superior reverse was created, designed by Edgar Fuller and modelled by Cecil Thomas. This floral pattern seems balanced and ordinary at first glance, but is in fact a very cunning and carefully thought-out pattern, the legend figuring as part of the overall layout.

Half-crowns (2s. 6d.)

Date	Mintage
VICTORIA (1837–1901)	
Young Head	
1839	—
1840	0·4
1841	0·04
1842	0·5
1843	0·5
1844	2·0
1845	2·2
1846	1·5
1848 ⎫ 1848/6 ⎭	0·4
1849	0·3
1850	0·5
1874	2·2
1875	1·1
1876	0·6
1877	0·4
1878	1·5
1880	1·3
1881	2·3
1882	0·8
1883	3·0
1884	1·6
1885	1·6
1886	0·9
1887	1·4

The half-crowns of the young Victoria are a pleasure to handle and a joy to study (see 1844 date on cover). Even in the lower grades these early pieces look superb, especially when toned. Technically there are six different types between 1839 and 1887, but for our purposes we will subdivide them into two groups 1839–50 and 1874–87. There was none issued between 1850 and 1874, despite many erroneous reports to the contrary.

I investigated over twenty coins with dates of 1861, 1866, 1868 and 1871, and all were proved to be fakes, in spite of the fact that the Royal Mint had in many instances advised their respective owners to the contrary.

Date	Mintage
Jubilee Head	
1887	Inc. in YH
1888	1·4
1889	4·8
1890	3·2
1891	2·3
1892	1·7
Old Head	
1893	1·8
1894	1·5
1895	1·8
1896	2·1
1897	1·7
1898	1·9
1899	2·9
1900	4·5
1901	1·5
EDWARD VII (1902–10)	
1902	1·3
1903	0·3
1904	0·7
1905	0·2
1906	2·9
1907	3·7

The first group are very well struck in high relief and have a medallic appearance. The post-1874 group are decidedly inferior and lack the character of the earlier coins.

Until the wild price spiralling in 1968/9, the half-crown would have ranked as the most widely collected of our 'silver' coinage. Before the 'price madness' set in it was not too difficult to build up a complete set from 1887 to date, in average condition, with the later dates virtually all in mint state. Today it is a different story, with even the commonest of dates withdrawn from circulation, premiums are being asked for virtually everything.

Uncirculated half-crowns of dates like 1903, 1904, 1905 are worth many times their weight in gold, pushed to unrealistic heights by dealers and speculators who should have known better.

Date	Mintage
1908	1·8
1909	3·0
1910	2·6

GEORGE V (1911–36)

1911	2·9
1912	4·7
1913	4·1
1914	18·3
1915	32·4
1916	29·5
1917	11·2
1918	29·1
1919	10·3
1920	18·0
1921	23·7
1922 Var I	
1922 Var II	16·4
1923	26·3
1924	5·9
1925	1·4
1926	
1926 ME	4·5
1927	6·9
1928	18·8
1929	17·6
1930	0·8

All the 1905 silver coins are scarce, but the half-crown is now quite rare. Rumour has it that they were shipped to the island of St. Helena in the Atlantic for circulation there. Perfect, unblemished specimens are very few and far between, the majority of known pieces being in 'fine' condition.

The occurrence of two world wars between the years listed here, did little to alter the character of the half-crown. Apart from two distinct changes in its metallic content, the reverse type remained constant. The first issue of George V are in fairly high relief, and the design suffers even after a minimal amount of wear. The post-1920 silver has the alarming habit of turning yellow on the raised surfaces when the copper content discolours in the atmosphere.

Date	Mintage
1931	11·3
1932	4·8
1933	10·3
1934	2·4
1935	7·0
1936	7·0

GEORGE VI (1937–52)

Date	Mintage
1937	9·1
1938	6·4
1939	15·5
1940	17·9
1941	15·8
1942	31·2
1943	15·5
1944	15·3
1945	19·8
1946	22·7
1947	21·9
1948	71·2
1949	28·3
1950	28·3
1951	9·0
1952	—

The attempts to alter this resulted in the new coinage of 1927. Certain of the 1926 coins were issued having been struck with the new obverse dies, creating what collectors have christened the 'Modified Effigy' variety. Incidentally, the two types of 1922 half-crown, which are not very important, can be distinguished by whether or not they have a groove between the crown and the shield on the reverse.

The so-called unique 1952 half-crown—it must qualify as Britain's most publicised coin. It was eventually sold in the U.S.A. for £2,200, after several major problems with its United Kingdom sale.

Half-crowns (2s. 6d.)—*continued*

Date	Mintage
ELIZABETH II (1953–)	
1953	3·9
1954	11·6
1955	23·6
1956	33·9
1957	34·2
1958	15·7
1959	9·0
1960	19·9
1961	25·9
1961	Polished Flan
1962	24·0
1963	17·6
1964	6·0
1965	9·8
1966	13·4
1967	18·9

Proof half-crowns were issued in the specimen sets for the years 1950, 1951, and 1953. These proof coins are occasionally offered by coin dealers when a set is 'broken', i.e. sold individually, coin by coin. The number of sets issued were 17,513; 20,000; 40,000 respectively, the first set being issued for numismatic purposes, the second for the Festival of Britain, and the third for the Coronation of Queen Elizabeth.

To date only one genuine 1952 half-crown has ever turned up and that fetched £2,200 in the U.S.A.

Double Florins (4s.)

Date	Mintage
VICTORIA (1837–1901)	

Jubilee Head

1887 Roman ⎫	483,347
1887 Arabic ⎭	
1888	243,340
1889	1·2m.
1890	782,146

The ungainly, rather point-less double florin was first issued in 1887, to be dis-continued in 1890. This was a completely new denomination and was often passed on to un-suspecting members of the public as the 'new type of crown' and was nicknamed 'the barmaid's nightmare' for just that reason.

Crowns (5s.)

Date	Mintage
VICTORIA (1837–1901)	

Young Head

1844 VIII	94,248
1845 VIII	159,192
1847 YH. XI	140,976
1847 Gothic	8,000
1853 Gothic	460

Jubilee Head

1887	273,000
1887	
1888	131,000
1889	1,800,000
1890	1,000,000
1891	566,000
1892	451,000

It would take a very deep purse to build-up a complete Crown collection as listed here from the beginning of Victoria's reign to date, with all the coins in mint state. There are four types of Vic-torian crown, the Young Head, Gothic, Jubilee, and Old Head issues, as shown here.

Crowns (5s.)—*continued*

Date	Mintage
Old Head	
1893 LVI } 1893 LVII	500,000
1894 LVII } 1894 LVIII	144,000
1895 LVIII } 1895 LIX	252,000
1896 LIX } 1896 LX	317,000
1897 LX } 1897 LXI	262,000
1898 LXI } 1898 LXII	161,000
1899 LXII } 1899 LXIII	166,000
1900 LXIII } 1900 LXIV	353,000
EDWARD VII (1902–10)	
1902	256,000

The Gothic crown is popularly considered to be one of the most beautiful coins ever made, the obverse having been designed by William Wyon and the reverse by W. Dyce. Apart from the Jubilee issue, the other three types carry a raised edge legend or inscription with the regnal year included. This in fact indicated the length of time the monarch had reigned when the coin was issued. Therefore the coins issued for circulation up to June in Victoria's case, e.g. 1893, bore the latin numerals LVI (56), while those issued after June were imparted with LVII (57). The 1902 crown continued this with the edge legend 'DECUS ET TUTAMEN. ANNO REGNI II', while the first type of George V's crowns had reeded edges.

143

Crowns (5s.)—*continued*

Date	Mintage
GEORGE V (1911–36)	
1927 (Proofs)	15,030
1928	9,034
1929	4,994
1930	4,847
1931	4,056
1932	2,395
1933	7,132
1934	932
1935	714,000
1935	2,500
1936	2,473
GEORGE VI (1937–52)	
1937	418,000
1937 Proofs	(26,402)
1951 Proofs	2m.
ELIZABETH II (1953–)	
1953	6 m.
1960	1 m.
1965	19·6 m.

1935 was George V's silver jubilee and the crown issued in that year deviated from the norm by the use of a symbolic St. George. The crowns of George VI were both superbly executed and above reproach, which is more than can be said for the coins of the present reign. The obverse of the 1953 coronation crown bears an unusual equestrian portrait of the queen in low relief. The reverse has the arms of England, Ireland, and Scotland separated by the rose, shamrock, thistle, and leek. The 1960 crown was issued for the British Exhibition in New York and the 1965, the last of the true English crowns, was issued as a tribute to Sir Winston Churchill.

GOLD COINAGE

Half-sovereigns

Date	Mintage	Date	Mintage
VICTORIA (1837–1901)		1864	1,758,490
Young Head		1865	1,834,750
1838	273,341	1866	2,058,776
1839	1,230	1867	992,795
1841	508,835	1869	1,861,764
1842	2,223,352	1870	1,159,544
1843	1,251,762	1871	2,062,970
1844	1,127,007	1872	3,248,627
1845	887,526	1873	1,927,050
1846	1,063,928	1874	1,884,432
1847	982,636	1875	516,240
1848	410,595	1876	2,785,187
1849	845,112	1878	2,081,941
1850	179,595	1879	35,201
1851	773,573	1880	1,009,049
1852	1,377,671	1883	2,870,457
1853	2,708,796	1884	1,133,756
1854	1,125,144	1885	4,468,871
1856	2,391,909		
1857	728,223	*Jubilee Head*	
1858	855,578	1887	871,770
1859	2,203,813	1890	2,266,023
1860	1,131,500	1891	1,079,286
1861	1,130,867	1892	13,680,486
1863	1,571,574	1893	4,426,625

Half-sovereigns—
continued

Date	Mintage
Old Head	
1893	Incl.
1894	3,794,591
1895	2,869;183
1896	2,946,605
1897	3,568,156
1898	2,868,527
1899	3,361,881
1900	4,307,372
1901	2,037,664

EDWARD VII (1901–10)

Date	Mintage
1902	{ 15,123 { 4,244,457
1903	2,522,057
1904	1,717,440
1905	3,023,993
1906	4,245,437
1907	4,233,421
1908	3,996,992
1909	4,010,715
1910	5,023,881

GEORGE V (1911–36)

Date	Mintage
1911	6,104,106
1912	6,224,316
1913	6,094,290
1914	7,251,124
1915	2,042,747

GEORGE VI (1937–52)

Date	Mintage
1937	5,501 Proofs

Sovereigns

Date	Mintage
VICTORIA (1837–1901)	
Young Head	
1838	2,718,694
1839	503,695
1841	124,054
1842	4,865,375
1843 Broad shield	} 5,981,968
1843 Narrow shield	
1844	3,000,445
1845	3,800,845
1846	3,802,947
1847	4,667,126
1848	2,246,701
1849	1,755,399
1850	1,402,039
1851	4,013,624

Sovereigns—*continued*

Date	Mintage	Date	Mintage
1852	8,053,435	1864	8,656,352
		1865	1,450,238
1853 W.W.* raised		1866	4,047,288
1853 W.W. incuse	10,597,993	1868	1,653,384
		1869	6,441,322
1854 W.W. raised		1870	2,189,960
1854 W.W. incuse	3,589,611	1871 Shield	8,767,250
		1872 Shield/ Die no.	
1855 W.W. raised		1872 Shield/ None	13,486,708
1855 W.W. incuse	8,448,482	1873 Shield	2,368,215
		1874 Shield	520,713
1856			
1856 small date	4,806,160	*New Reverse*	
1857	4,495,748	1871 St. G.†	Incl. above
1858	803,234	1872 St. G.	Incl. above
1859		1873 St. G.	Incl. above
1859 small date	1,547,603	1874 St. G.	Incl. above
1860	2,555,958	1876	3,318,866
1861	7,624,736	1878	1,091,275
1862	7,836,413	1879	20,013
1863 No die no.		1880 No initials	3,650,080
1863 Die no.	5,921,669	1884	1,769,635
		1885	717,723

* W.W. = Engraver's Initials, William Wyon.
† St. G. = St. George and the Dragon reverse.

Sovereigns—*continued*

Date	Mintage
Jubilee Head	
1887	1,111,280
1888	2,277,424
1889	7,257,455
1890	6,529,887
1891	6,329,476
1892	7,104,720
Old Head	
1893	6,898,260
1894	3,782,611
1895	2,285,317
1896	3,334,065
1898	4,361,347
1899	7,515,978
1900	10,846,741
1901	1,578,948

EDWARD VII (1902–10)

Date	Mintage
1902	4,737,796
1903	8,888,627
1904	10,041,369
1905	5,910,403
1906	10,466,981
1907	18,458,663
1908	11,729,006

Date	Mintage
1909	12,157,099
1910	22,379,624

GEORGE V (1911–36)

1911	30,044,105
1912	30,317,921
1913	24,539,672
1914	11,501,117
1915	20,295,280
1916	1,554,120
1917	1,014,714
1925	4,406,431

GEORGE VI (1937–52)

1937	5,501 Proofs

ELIZABETH II (1953–   )

1957	2,072,000
1958	8,700,140
1959	1,358,228
1962	3,000,000
1963	7,400,000
1964	3,000,000
1965	3,800,000
1966	7,005,000
1967	5,000,000
1968	4,203,000

Two Pounds

Date	Mintage
VICTORIA (1837–1901)	
1887 Jubilee	91,345
Proof	797
1893 Old Head	52,212
Proof	773
EDWARD VII (1902–10)	
1902 Normal	45,807
Proof	8,066
GEORGE V (1911–36)	
1911 Proof only	2,812
GEORGE VI (1937–52)	
1937 Proof only	5,501

Five Pounds

Date	Mintage
VICTORIA (1837–1901)	
1839 Y.H. Patterns only	
1887 Jubilee	53,844
Proof	797
1893 Old Head	20,405
Proof	773
EDWARD VII (1902–10)	
1902 Normal	34,911
Proof	8,066
GEORGE V (1911–36)	
1911 Proof only	2,812
GEORGE VI (1936–52)	
1937 Proof only	5,501

ABBREVIATIONS

RE	RE for REG.
W.W. RAISED	Engraver's initials raised on truncation.
No W.W.	No engraver's initials (W. Wyon).
BD	Beaded border.
TH	Toothed border.
H	Heaton Mint-mark ⎱
KN	Kings Norton ⎰ Birmingham.
	Mint-mark ⎰
YH	Young head ⎱
OH	Old head ⎰ Victoria.
JH	Jubilee head ⎰
Normal	Bright finish ⎱ 1897 Farthing.
Black	Black finish ⎰
SM date	Small Date.
No SIG	No engraver's signature.
SIG	Engraver's signature present.
1851 'DOTS'	Seven incuse dots on or above the shield (halfpence).
Low Tide	(1902) Horizon only half-way up Britannia's leg (Penny and Halfpenny).
Plain 4	No bar on end horizontal ⎱ (Penny).
Cr'slt 4	With bar (crosslet) ⎰
'73 Type	Type of 1873.

New 1881	New portrait.
2 MM 1895	Trident 2 millimetres from 'P' of 'PENNY'.
ME	1926 Modified Effigy, i.e. new portrait of King.
R.R. 1868	R instead of B, i.e. RRITANNIAR—error.
DIE NO	Small die number over date—to measure life of die.
DR 1878	Error—DRITANNIAR (Sixpence).
New 1927	New type.
SH	Small head.
E	English shilling.
S	Scottish shilling.
	(With Elizabeth 1s. 'E' have 3 leopards in shield, S have one LION).
xxri	1881 error in date, it should be xxxi.
FDC	Fleur de coin, i.e. Perfect in every respect.
VAR I	Variety I—No groove between Crown/Shield.
VAR II	Variety II—Groove exists between Crown/Shield.
Flan	Blank, unminted coin.
ROMAN } ARABIC	Variety in type of 1 in the date (4s.).
1·2m.	1,200,000 (mintage figures).
LVI } LVII } VIII	Regnal years, on edge legend of crowns.

PROOF	Specially struck from polished dies and flans.
GOTHIC	The bust of Victoria in 'Gothic style'.
f	Denotes face value.
Raised Edge Proof	Edge legend in relief as opposed to incuse.
1851 'D'	D of DEI over (Farthing).
1887 WD 6*d*	Withdrawn type.
1887 WR	Wreath type.
E over N	E of REGINA over N (1843 ½-farthing).

MAUNDY MONEY

The Maundy Money ceremony originates from the Last Supper of Our Lord when He delivered the Mandatum to His Disciples.

The first evidence of the Maundy in Britain was when St. Augustine reintroduced Christianity in A.D. 597. The first record of a Monarch distributing money to the poor occurs

Reverse of the 1937 Maundy fourpence, a coin never issued for circulation (see text).

in the reign of King John, 1199–1216. However, it is not until Elizabeth I's reign that we have any documented proof of the money being allocated in specific amounts.

A small quantity of silver bullion was assigned to the Queen annually and increased with each successive year. This custom suggested that as the monarch aged, the amount of silver pence given increased accordingly. By complying with this, so tradition evolved and a custom became accepted.

The Tudors and Stuarts gave great prominence to the Maundy ceremony, meticulously observing traditional charity, in the form of both Maundy coins and food and clothing. Today the ceremony is regularly held by Elizabeth II, at one of our famous cathedrals, on the Maundy Thursday of each year. According to the Queen's age (43 years in 1969), forty-three men and forty-three women are handed as many silver pence each, plus additional money in lieu of food and clothing.

The Maundy coins are specially struck in silver denominations of 1d., 2d., 3d., and 4d. The silver content is 92·5%. The sets are made up in purses to a total of £4 18s. 6d. for the men, to £4 8s. 6d. for the women. The difference in amount is based on the assumption that women need less money for clothing, an ironic assumption by modern standards. This is made up as follows (for men):

	£	s.	d.
In a red leather purse with white thongs—			
(1) For the redemption of the Sovereign's gown, worn on the day of Distribution	0	0	
(2) Allowance in lieu of provisions	1	10	0
In a white leather purse with red thongs—			
Silver Maundy pence totalling 43 pence		3	6
In a white leather purse with green thongs			
Allowance in lieu of clothing	2	5	0
	4	18	6

Strangely enough, the Maundy coins are still legal tender at their original face-value. Undoubtedly, this originates from the past custom; as the current collector value is many hundred times this value. These coins, annually issued in sets since the reign of Charles II, follow the other obverses of the coins in each of the reigns in which they were struck, and are greatly sought after. Dealers are known to go to great lengths to obtain a small allocation from an average 1,200 issued annually. It is reported that when the ceremony was at Westminster Abbey one dealer joined the 'washer-uppers' in the refreshment kitchen in order to make contact with one fortunate who had received some coins. One may well ask if charity begins at home!

CORGI MINI-BOOKS

continued

continued

All these books are available at your local bookshop or newsagent; or can be ordered direct from the publisher. Just tick the titles you want and fill in the form below.

CORGI BOOKS, Cash Sales Department, J. Barnicoat (Falmouth) Ltd., P.O. Box 11, Falmouth, Cornwall.
Please send cheque or postal order. No currency, and allow 6d. per book to cover the cost of postage and packing in U.K., 9d. per copy overseas.

NAME ....

ADDRESS ....

....